VOLUME 137

Turks and Caicos Islands

Paul G. Boultbee

Compiler

CLIO PRESS

OXFORD, ENGLAND · SANTA BARBARA, CALIFORNIA
DENVER, COLORADO

British Library Cataloguing in Publication Data

Boultbee, Paul G.
Turks and Caicos Islands (World bibliographical series; v.137)
I. Title   II. Series
016.97296

ISBN 1-85109-162-9

Clio Press Ltd.,
55 St. Thomas' Street,
Oxford OX1 1JG, England.

ABC-CLIO,
130 Cremona Drive,
Santa Barbara,
CA 93117, USA.

Designed by Bernard Crossland.
Typeset by Columns Design and Production Services, Reading, England.
Printed and bound in Great Britain by
Billing and Sons Ltd., Worcester.

Turks and Caicos Islands

WORLD BIBLIOGRAPHICAL SERIES

General Editors:
Robert G. Neville (Executive Editor)
John J. Horton

Robert A. Myers   Ian Wallace
Hans H. Wellisch   Ralph Lee Woodward, Jr.

John J. Horton is Deputy Librarian of the University of Bradford and currently Chairman of its Academic Board of Studies in Social Sciences. He has maintained a longstanding interest in the discipline of area studies and its associated bibliographical problems, with special reference to European Studies. In particular he has published in the field of Icelandic and of Yugoslav studies, including the two relevant volumes in the World Bibliographical Series.

Robert A. Myers is Associate Professor of Anthropology in the Division of Social Sciences and Director of Study Abroad Programs at Alfred University, Alfred, New York. He has studied post-colonial island nations of the Caribbean and has spent two years in Nigeria on a Fulbright Lectureship. His interests include international public health, historical anthropology and developing societies. In addition to *Amerindians of the Lesser Antilles: a bibliography* (1981), *A Resource Guide to Dominica, 1493–1986* (1987) and numerous articles, he has compiled the World Bibliographical Series volumes on *Dominica* (1987), *Nigeria* (1989) and *Ghana* (1991).

Ian Wallace is Professor of German at the University of Bath. A graduate of Oxford in French and German, he also studied in Tübingen, Heidelberg and Lausanne before taking teaching posts at universities in the USA, Scotland and England. He specializes in contemporary German affairs, especially literature and culture, on which he has published numerous articles and books. In 1979 he founded the journal *GDR Monitor*, which he continues to edit under its new title *German Monitor*.

Hans H. Wellisch is Professor emeritus at the College of Library and Information Services, University of Maryland. He was President of the American Society of Indexers and was a member of the International Federation for Documentation. He is the author of numerous articles and several books on indexing and abstracting, and has published *The Conversion of Scripts* and *Indexing and Abstracting: an International Bibliography*. He also contributes frequently to *Journal of the American Society for Information Science, The Indexer* and other professional journals.

Ralph Lee Woodward, Jr. is Chairman of the Department of History at Tulane University, New Orleans, where he has been Professor of History since 1970. He is the author of *Central America, a Nation Divided*, 2nd ed. (1985), as well as several monographs and more than sixty scholarly articles on modern Latin America. He has also compiled volumes in the World Bibliographical Series on *Belize* (1980), *Nicaragua* (1983), and *El Salvador* (1988). Dr. Woodward edited the Central American section of the *Research Guide to Central America and the Caribbean* (1985) and is currently editor of the Central American history section of the *Handbook of Latin American Studies*.

THE WORLD BIBLIOGRAPHICAL SERIES

This series, which is principally designed for the English speaker, will eventually cover every country (and many of the world's principal regions), each in a separate volume comprising annotated entries on works dealing with its history, geography, economy and politics; and with its people, their culture, customs, religion and social organization. Attention will also be paid to current living conditions – housing, education, newspapers, clothing, etc.– that are all too often ignored in standard bibliographies; and to those particular aspects relevant to individual countries. Each volume seeks to achieve, by use of careful selectivity and critical assessment of the literature, an expression of the country and an appreciation of its nature and national aspirations, to guide the reader towards an understanding of its importance. The keynote of the series is to provide, in a uniform format, an interpretation of each country that will express its culture, its place in the world, and the qualities and background that make it unique. The views expressed in individual volumes, however, are not necessarily those of the publisher.

VOLUMES IN THE SERIES

For my family
with love and gratitude
for all your support
through the years

Contents

Contents

Introduction

The Turks and Caicos Islands, made up of two groups of islands lying to the southeast of the Bahamas, cover a surface area of 193 square miles and support a population of approximately 13,000. The Turks Islands, said to be named after a species of cactus whose scarlet flowers resemble a Turkish fez, consist of two inhabited islands – Grand Turk and Salt Cay, six uninhabited cays and a large number of rocks. The principal islands of the Caicos group are South Caicos, East Caicos, Middle (or Grand) Caicos, North Caicos, Providenciales and West Caicos. The name Caicos probably comes from the Spanish 'cayos' which means cays.

The islands were first discovered by Juan Ponce de Leon (c. 1460-1521) in 1512 though there is increasing evidence that Christopher Columbus (1451-1506) may have made his first landfall in the New World in the Turks and Caicos Islands and not the Bahamas. Archaeological evidence also indicates that, like the Bahamas, the Turks and Caicos Islands were probably inhabited by Arawak Indians (known as Lucayans in this region) at the time of discovery but, again like the Bahamas, these inhabitants were taken into slavery by the Spanish and had disappeared from the islands by 1520.

Salt rakers from Bermuda were the first Europeans to occupy the islands. Beginning as early as 1678, they came regularly from March to November which was the salt raking season. Bahamian, Bermudian, Spanish, French and British rivalry over the prospering salt trade resulted in numerous invasions and evictions throughout the eighteenth century. However, it wasn't until the 1780s that more permanent settlements were established. At this time Loyalists from the southern United States began to settle in the Bahamas and the Turks and Caicos Islands after the American War of Independence.

The plantations they established, chiefly in the Caicos Islands group, were not as successful as those they had left behind and, following the abolition of slavery in the 1830s, the planters left the islands. Their land fell into the possession of the former slaves.

In 1799 the islands were placed under the stewardship of the British Colonial Administration. The Bahamas was given jurisdiction over the islands and they in turn were given representation in the Bahamas House of Assembly. This arrangement lasted until 1848 when, following an ongoing dispute with Bahamian salt proprietors, the inhabitants of the islands requested, and were granted, a separate charter. The Turks and Caicos Islands then became a separate colony with an elective Legislative Board and a President to administer the government.

By 1873 the Legislative Council petitioned Her Majesty for the islands to be annexed to Jamaica. The Order in Council of 1873 made provision for this and for the constitution of a Legislative Board. It also provided for a Commissioner as ex-officio President of the Board which had full legislative and budgetary powers. However, ordinances required the assent of the Governor of Jamaica before becoming law. Under these changes, the Turks and Caicos Islands remained a dependency of Jamaica until 1959.

The Turks and Caicos Islands (Constitution) Order in Council 1959 provided for a new constitution which was brought into operation on 4 July 1959. Under this new constitution, the Governor of the Islands was constituted (the Governor of Jamaica was also Governor of the Islands) and the office of Commissioner was replaced by the office of the Administrator. The Legislative Board was replaced by the Legislative Assembly consisting of the Administrator as President, two or three official members appointed by the Governor, two or three nominated non-official members appointed by the Governor and nine members elected on a constituency basis by universal adult suffrage. An Executive Council was also introduced. It consisted of the Administrator, two official members, one nominated member and two elected members.

The next constitutional change occurred in 1962. Following Jamaican independence, the island group became a British Crown Colony. The post of Governor was abolished and the powers formerly exercised by the Governor were now exercised by the Administrator. Within three years, new talks between representatives of the United Kingdom, the Bahamas and the Turks and Caicos Islands saw the Governor of the Bahamas also becoming the Governor of the Turks and Caicos Islands under the Turks and Caicos Islands (Constitution) Order in Council 1965, though the post of Administrator remained.

In 1969 a new constitution came into force on 18 June which provided for an Administrator and a State Council consisting of a Speaker, three official members, not less than two nor more than three nominated members and nine elected members. The powers previously held by the Governor and Commander-in-Chief of the Bahamas transferred to Governor, Supreme Court and Court of Appeal of the Turks and Caicos Islands. The office of Administrator was abolished and replaced by the post of Governor.

Yet another constitution was introduced on 30 August 1976 through the Turks and Caicos Islands (Constitution) Order 1976. This constitution provided for a separate executive advisory council to the Governor with provision for a Chief Minister and not more than three ministers with responsibility for the business of government exercised in accordance with policies decided by the Executive Council. The 1976 constitution remained in effect until 1986 when, following a public inquiry to investigate allegations of arson, corruption and maladministration, the Executive Council was dissolved and Ministerial government suspended. It was determined that the Chief Minister and several leading ministers had indulged in unconstitutional behaviour, political discrimination and administrative malpractice and were unfit to exercise ministerial responsibility. Consequently, resignations were received from the Chief Minister, the Minister of Health and Education, and the Minister of Public Works and Utilities. The inquiry also concluded that the leaders of the opposition were unfit to hold public office. Through an Order to Council, the Governor replaced the Executive Council with an interim Advisory Council, of which he was the Chairman. It was not until March 1988 that, following a General Election, the Turks and Caicos Islands returned to Ministerial government.

It has not always been other islands within the Caribbean with which the inhabitants of the Turks and Caicos have wished to associate themselves. As early as 1917 there has been a move to establish links with Canada. The biggest push for such a move came in 1974 when a Canadian Member of Parliament proposed that Canada should adopt the islands. This was followed by further questions in the Canadian House of Commons in 1976. Very little, if anything, has been done about such links but the impetus is still there. A 1986 Turks and Caicos poll showed that ninety per cent of the inhabitants favoured some kind of association with Canada.

Until the 1960s, the salt industry was the mainstay of the Turks and Caicos economy, but unprofitable production techniques and international competition led to the industry's collapse after almost three hundred years. Various other industries have been introduced but very few have actually succeeded. The cultivation of cotton and tobacco in the seventeenth and eighteenth centuries eventually failed as did pineapple production after its introduction in 1883. Cotton production was revived in the early twentieth century but failed in the 1920s after continual droughts and the appearance of the destructive boll weevil. The production and export of sisal fibre was a major industry until the mid 1960s, but ceased following mass migration of Caicos Islanders to the Bahamas and increased world production of higher quality fibre. Today, the islands' economy depends primarily on offshore banking and insurance and a growing tourist trade. There is also a small industry devoted to the harvesting of seafood for export.

Drug-trafficking has become a problem in the Turks and Caicos Islands and has, unfortunately, made its presence felt at the highest levels. In 1985, the Chief Minister was arrested in Miami, Florida, and charged with conspiracy to import narcotics into the United States. Arrested along with him were the Minister of Trade and Development and a member of the Legislative Council. Both the Chief Minister and the Minister of Trade and Development were subsequently convicted and sentenced to prison terms.

The history of the Turks and Caicos Islands has been marked by frequent changes in leadership – perhaps not always in the best interests of the islanders. And life on these not-always-idyllic tropical islands can be harsh. However, Turks and Caicos Islanders must look to the future. Tourism appears to be the key to better times but other means to diversify the economy must not be ignored.

The Bibliography

This is probably the first bibliography strictly devoted to materials about the Turks and Caicos Islands in a variety of subject areas. Prior to this, the Turks and Caicos were invariably included in bibliographies about the Bahamas and information on the islands was also often found in books and articles about the Bahamas. The 305 entries have been grouped into twenty-five categories, plus sub-categories, which are similar to those found in other volumes of the World Bibliographical Series. Some special categories have been added to reflect Turks and Caicos circumstances. There is a separate subcategory under 'Prehistory and Archaeology' to document the important Molasses Reef wreck excavations. Some investigators believe that this shipwreck could be Christopher Columbus' *Pinta*. There are also history categories to highlight the Turks and Caicos Islands' relationships with Bermuda, the Bahamas and Jamaica. Proposed association with Canada is listed separately under 'Foreign Relations'. There is no literature from the Turks and Caicos Islands but literature set in the region has been included.

Readers familiar with the World Bibliographical Series will note that several usual categories are not included in this volume. This is because no items could be found in these subject areas. The Turks and Caicos Islands are little-known and little-studied; therefore, as many items as possible have been included. For the most part, only inconsequential travel articles have been excluded. The bibliography is certainly not exhaustive, but it is as complete as possible.

With one exception, all sections are arranged with the most recent items listed first. Items under the category, 'History. 1500 to the Present' have been arranged chronologically by date of content not date of publication. Two or more items published in the same year have been listed alphabetically by the first major word in the title.

The bibliography includes books, journal articles, dissertations and some government documents. Some of the items may be difficult for researchers to find, but have been included here because of the general lack of information about the islands. Many are available at the Victoria Public Library on Grand Turk (Front Street, Grand Turk, Turks and Caicos Islands, British West Indies). Other items can be found in the Library of the Royal Commonwealth Society (Northumberland Avenue, London WC2N 5BJ, England), the Library of Congress (Washington, DC 20540) and in a number of major university libraries in both Canada and the United States. Addresses for unusual items have been included in the annotations.

Acknowledgements

I would like to express my thanks to all those who have helped me in the compilation of this bibliography. I was able to see a great deal of material at the Victoria Public Library on Grand Turk and wish to thank the former Assistant Librarian, Ms. Sharon Taylor, and the rest of the Library staff for their help. Miss T. A. Barringer, Librarian of the Royal Commonwealth Society, provided me with valuable information about the RCS's collection of Turks and Caicos material and I am grateful for her assistance. Mr. Brian Riggs, Curator of the Turks and Caicos National Museum, was also most helpful in bringing a number of items to my attention and providing background information.

Special thanks to my wife, Glynis, who once again has given me support and encouragement. As always, I value her thoughtful suggestions and sound advice.

Paul G. Boultbee
August 1991

The Country and its People

1 **The Caribbean handbook, 1990.**
Edited by Jeremy Taylor. St. John's: FT Caribbean, 1990. 260p.
31 maps. bibliog.
This handbook is divided into two sections. The first contains articles on a variety of subjects including banking and offshore finance, telecommunications, tourism, investment, foreign relations, manufacturing, agriculture, the media, energy, currency, public holidays, languages, airlines and shipping. The second section consists of articles on each of the different countries in the Caribbean region. The article on the Turks and Caicos Islands contains a great deal of information about population, climate, politics, travel and accommodation, telecommunications, the business environment, government, the economy and a list of key historical dates. Useful for making comparisons with other Caribbean islands.

2 **The Turks and Caicos Islands: a geographical note.**
Michael Fergus. *Geography*, vol. 76, no. 326 (Jan. 1990), p. 66-67.
Fergus' article contains some historical and geographical information but his primary focus is economic development and the future. He sees tourism and the offshore finance business as being potential future successes for the islands. He indicates that labour shortages and the subsequent importation of Haitian labourers, illegal Haitian immigration and poor communications with the outside world as being problems with which the islands will have to contend.

3 **The Turks and Caicos Islands: lands of discovery.**
Amelia Smithers. London: Macmillan Caribbean, 1990. 88p. 3 maps.
bibliog.
In this handbook/guidebook, Smithers presents information on the natural and social history of the islands. There are also chapters on the two main island groups, the Turks Islands and the Caicos Islands and a chapter on the other scattered cays. There are detailed descriptions of Grand Turk and Providenciales.

4 **Our country, the Turks and Caicos Islands.**
Turks and Caicos Islands. Education Department. London: Macmillan Caribbean, 1989. 168p. 11 maps.

This is the first book produced specifically for the children of the Turks and Caicos Islands. It was written by twelve teachers and education officers in workshops sponsored by the United Nations Development Programme to assist the teaching of Social Studies in primary and secondary schools, though its main target is eight to ten-year-olds. The book's forty-six chapters cover geography, history, industries (both past and present), tourism, communications, money and trade, government, culture and the problems facing the country's growth. Questions and exercises follow each chapter. This is an excellent introduction for school children.

5 **Turks and Caicos Islands.**
In: *Worldmark encyclopedia of the nations.* New York: Worldmark Press, 1988. 7th ed. p. 271-74.

This brief outline of the Turks and Caicos Islands provides basic information under fifty different categories including topography, climate, population, transportation, history, economy, agriculture, health, education and the media.

6 **The turned-on, tuned-in, dropped-out characters of Turks and Caicos.**
William Deverell. *Destinations*, vol. 3, no. 4 (Sept. 1988), p. 30-35, 37, 39-41.

This is a delightful and informative article offering a description of the islands as well as information on history and politics. Deverell also touches on the association with Canada proposed by various Canadian and Turks and Caicos politicians and offers insights into the feelings of some island residents about this proposal. A slightly abridged version of this article appeared in the January 1989 issue of *Reader's Digest* (Canadian edition, vol. 134, no. 801, p. 30-34) under the title, 'A not-much-doin' place, man'.

7 **The mongrel islands.**
Conger Beasley. *North American Review*, vol. 272, no. 4 (Dec. 1987), p. 4-9.

In describing a region that no one wants, with no exploitable resources and little promise for the future, Beasley paints a picture of lethargy and stagnation. He calls the Turks and Caicos Islands 'mongrel' because of the influences of Spanish, French and British occupations on the society and culture, and describes this mongrelization as 'a cultural reality of many Caribbean countries composed . . . of contrasting European and African influences' (p. 6). Beasley sees very little promise for the Turks and Caicos Islands.

8 **Between the devil and a deep blue sea.**
Terry Coleman. *Guardian*, (Feb. 15, 1986), p. 17.

In this sardonic and eclectic three-column newspaper article, Coleman provides amusing and surprisingly unified comments on drug trafficking, Columbus' first landfall in the New World, the stamp industry in the Turks and Caicos Islands and Providenciales' Club Med.

9 **Outposts.**
   Simon Winchester.   London: Hodder & Stoughton, 1985. 316p. 16 maps.
   bibliog.

In this work, Winchester describes his visits to all of the remaining colonies in the British Empire. In his comments on the Turks and Caicos Islands (p. 202-10), he looks at the islands' history and the present conditions. Winchester's book is an amusing and, at times, nostalgic look at the remnants, mostly islands, of the British Empire which dot the globe.

10 **South America, Central America, and the Caribbean.**
   London: Europa Publications, 1985-. biennial.

This biennial is a very good quick-reference book for all countries in South and Central America and the Caribbean. There are articles which provide background material on the region and information on regional organizations. Entries for each country include statistics as well as information on history, politics and government, religion, the media, finance and banking, trade and industry, tourism and education. The entry for the Turks and Caicos Islands is brief but provides a useful overview.

11 **Turks and Caicos Islands: the Caribbean's secret.**
   W. John Redman.   *The Caribbean & West Indies Chronicle*,
   supplement (June/July 1983), p. i-xv.

Redman has written two articles: 'Staying with Britain. . .', which examines the islands' history and politics, and 'Well placed for development?', which looks at the islands' strategic geographic position and future potential in the areas of tourism, offshore finances, fishing and light manufacturing. There is also a statistical, fact-filled section in the supplement.

12 **Caribbean backwaters.**
   Ian Brown.   *Equinox*, vol. 1, no. 3 (May/June 1982), p. 84-104, 106,
   108.

Brown provides a look at the history and politics of the islands along with comments on tourist growth and development and the increasing drug trade. He also comments at length on the tensions between whites and blacks due not to the white presence in the islands but rather to the white absence – the refusal of whites to take part in the life of the black community.

13 **Danger in paradise.**
   Anthony Summers.   *Sunday Times Magazine*, (July 11, 1982), p. 16-17,
   19, 21-22, 25.

Following an outline of the islands' history and the frustrations with development and the British administration, Summers discusses the 1980 election, the new government of Chief Minister Norman Saunders and Saunders' alleged involvement with the drug trade. Summers is also very concerned with the close proximity of Cuba and the problems that could result if communism were to gain any sort of foothold.

14 **Secrets taken with a pinch of salt.**
Linda Christmas. *Guardian*, (Oct. 18, 1978), p. 16.
Christmas discusses several major problems confronting the Turks and Caicos Islands: lack of finances, neglect by Great Britain, the collapse of the salt industry, lack of tourism, and the rise in the drug trade.

15 **Turks and Caicos: a case of neglect?**
Geoffrey Cooper. *Commonwealth*, vol. 21 (Aug./Sept. 1978), p. 10-11.
Cooper discusses the lack of concern on the part of Great Britain's Foreign and Commonwealth Office, the lack of confidence in the future of the islands as expressed by some investors, and the frustration experienced by many of the islanders. He also points out that there is excellent potential for tourism.

16 **Caribbean year book.**
Toronto: Caribook, 1977/78-. annual.
This annual was first published in 1926/27 under the title, *West Indies and Caribbean year book* and is a very good quick-reference work for the Turks and Caicos Islands as well as for all other countries in the Caribbean region. It includes information on history, topography, climate, population, government, public and social services, public utilities, communications, natural resources, industries, finance, trade and commerce, diplomatic and consular offices, newspapers and periodicals. There is also a business directory.

17 **Profile of the Turks and Caicos Islands.**
Colin Rickards. *Caribbean Business News*, vol. 8, no. 6 (March 1977), p. 10-13.
This four-page article contains a number of shorter sections which give a great deal of basic information about the islands. It has been written primarily for the businessperson. Rickards provides a number of vital statistics, some historical background, descriptions of the major islands and information on the economy and investment potential.

18 **The Bahamas.**
George Hunte. London: Batsford, 1975. 200p. map. bibliog.
Like Craton's *A history of the Bahamas* (q.v.), Hunte's book provides some references to the Turks and Caicos Islands. There are general descriptions of the islands, as well as some information about history and geography.

19 **Turks and Caicos Islands outline development plan.**
Shankland Cox and Associates. London: Shankland Cox & Associates, 1971. 2 vols.
This two-volume document, consisting of a planning and policy report and a technical report, was prepared for the Overseas Development Administration of the Foreign and Commonwealth Office. It is intended to be a guideline for future development including consideration of alternative methods of development and advice on the islands' infrastructure requirements, legislation, institutional structure and implementation.

20   L'il orphan islands.
     Terry Johnson King.   *Travel*, vol. 122 (Nov. 1964), p. 61-62, 64, 66, 68.
     King takes a fascinating and delightful look at the Turks and Caicos Islands in the mid-1960s.

21   The Turks and Caicos Islands: some impressions of an English visitor.
     Doreen Collins.   *Caribbean Quarterly*, vol. 7, no. 3 (Dec. 1961),
     p. 163-67.
     Collins begins this article with a look at the history of the Turks and Caicos Islands focusing on the early settlers: salt rakers from Bermuda and Loyalists from Georgia. She shows how they influenced the attitudes and lifestyles of twentieth century islanders. Collins also discusses the salt industry, its problems and decline; the political future of the islands; and the problems related to tourism. A similar but less substantial article by Collins, entitled 'Turks and Caicos: unknown islands in the sun', appeared in the June 1961 issue of *New Commonwealth* (vol. 39, no. 6, p. 377-78).

22   Turks and Caicos Islands report.
     Great Britain. Colonial Office. London: HMSO, 1946-. annual.
     These annual reports provide a wealth of textual and statistical information about the following topics: finance, banking and commerce, education and health, agriculture, industry and labour, geography and history, legislation, justice and crime, communications, social services and population.

23   The Turks and Caicos Islands, British West Indies.
     Theodoor Hendrik Nikolaas de Booy.   *Geographical Review*, vol. 6,
     no. 1 (July 1918), p. 37-51.
     De Booy has written a wide ranging article which provides a great deal of background information. He begins with early settlement and history and then discusses the islands as two separate groups. First, he describes the Turks Islands, particularly Grand Turk, as well as Salt Cay and other cays, and provides information on the salt industry. Second, he investigates the Caicos Islands. He provides descriptions of North, South, East, West, and Grand Caicos Islands and Providenciales Island. De Booy also deals with sponges and conch as both fauna and the basis for industry, as well as the islands' climate and geology.

24   The handbook of the Turks and Caicos Islands: being a compendium of
     history, statistics and general information concerning the Islands from
     their discovery to the present time.
     J. Henry Pusey.   Kingston: Colonial Publishing, 1906. 2nd ed. 144p.
     map.
     Pusey, a Baptist minister on Grand Turk Island from 1880 to 1910, covers a wide variety of topics. His handbook provides a fascinating view of the Turks and Caicos Islands at the turn of the century. The handbook is divided into ten parts which provide information on such areas and topics as general and constitutional history, vital statistics, the salt and fibre industries, imports and exports, education, wrecks and whaling, and associations and clubs. Pusey also provides lists of government officials and a description of the islands along with a vast array of trivia which makes for fascinating reading. A short appendix provides some information on the Bahamas,

Bermuda, Cuba, Haiti and San Domingo. The first edition was published in 1897 (Kingston: Mortimer C. DeSouza. 163p.). There do not appear to have been any editions after 1906.

25 Account of Turks Island.

The Gentleman's Magazine, vol. 34 (Sept. 1764), p. 437.

This brief description of Grand Turk Island and the life of a salt-raker is one of the earliest to be found. It is particularly useful for the contemporary account given.

Geography

General

26 **A historical geography of the British colonies.**
Charles Prestwood Lucas. Oxford: Clarendon, 1887-1920. 7 vols.
Volume two (1905) contains information on the Turks and Caicos Islands. Lucas discusses history, climate, population, religion, agriculture and industry.

27 **An elementary class-book of the geography and history of the Turks and Caicos Islands.**
J. Henry Pusey. London: Elliot Stock, 1887. 46p.
This fascinating and still useful geography/history is divided into three major sections: physical geography, providing excellent descriptions; political geography; and history. Because this book was originally written to be used in the schools, Pusey has also appended questions for teacher/student use. There are two major drawbacks: the book is too brief and it is now rather difficult to find in major libraries.

28 **On the physical geography of, and the distribution of terrestrial mollusca in, the Bahama Islands.**
Thomas Bland. *Annals of the Lyceum of Natural History*, vol. 10 (1873), p. 311-24.
In the first half of this article, Bland describes the banks and islands of this region including the Turks and Caicos Islands Bank. He also gives some information about the geology of the area. Bland goes on to provide information, including locations, of twenty species of operculate land molluscs and sixty species of inoperculate land molluscs, and discusses their distribution throughout the West Indies.

Climate

29 Hurricanes of the Caribbean and adjacent regions, 1492-1800.
Jose Carlos Millas. Miami, Florida: Academy of the Arts and Sciences of the Americas, 1968. 328p. map. bibliog.

In this fascinating study, Millas examines contemporary documents pertaining to 308 reported hurricanes which allegedly occurred in the Caribbean between 1492 and 1800. He concludes that forty-five reported cases lack sufficient evidence to be considered true hurricanes. While Fassig (q.v.) looks at hurricanes in a general sense in his *Hurricanes of the West Indies*, Millas examines individual hurricanes in some detail.

30 Hurricanes of the West Indies.
Oliver Lanard Fassig. Washington, DC: Government Printing Office, 1913. 28p. 17 maps. (US Dept. of Agriculture. Weather Bureau. Bulletin X. W.B., 487).

In this report, Fassig concentrates on those storms which swept through the Caribbean between 1876 and 1911. He concludes that eighty-eight per cent of the hurricanes appear in August, September and October and have an average duration of six days. He also provides information on their origins and movements. The maps trace all of the hurricanes under examination. Fassig also pays particular attention to the devastating hurricane of 7-20 August 1899.

31 Climate of the Bahama Islands.
Oliver Lanard Fassig. In: *The Bahama Islands*. George Burbank Shattuck. New York: Macmillan, 1905, p. 111-25.

Fassig provides an introduction to the climate of the region, including the Turks and Caicos Islands, as well as specific information on temperature, relative humidity, rainfall, wind direction and velocity, thunderstorms and hurricanes. There are three maps in this chapter showing hurricane trails from 1878 to 1903. There are another three similar maps elsewhere in the volume.

32 West Indian hurricanes.
Edward Bennett Garriott. Washington, DC: Weather Bureau, 1900. 69p. (U.S. Dept. of Agriculture. Weather Bureau. Bulletin H. W.B., 232).

This report reviews the writings of the more prominent meteorologists of the nineteenth century insofar as they refer to tropical storms of the North Atlantic and presents a chronological list of West Indian storms from 1493 to 1900. There are also descriptions of some of the more important hurricanes.

Maps and atlases

33   **The atlas of Central America and the Caribbean.**
Diagram Group.   New York: Macmillan; London: Collier Macmillan,
1985. 144p. 91 maps. bibliog.

This atlas is divided into three sections: introduction/overview, Central American
nations, and Caribbean nations. For each nation examined, the editors provide a text
discussing history, land use, population, health and education, social welfare,
government and politics, and the economy. There are also a detailed physical map, a
picture of the national flag and seal, and basic statistical data. Where appropriate,
there are charts and tables for such elements as gross national product, imports and
exports, land use, crops, and climate.

34   **A comparison of the old and later charts of the Turks Islands.**
Henry Brougham Guppy.   In: *Plants, seeds, and currents in the West
Indies and Azores*. Henry Brougham Guppy. London: Williams &
Norgate, 1917, p. 489-91.

Guppy's work is based on the examination of two charts – a French chart from a survey
conducted in 1753, with improvements from observations in 1770 and eventually
published in 1794, and a British Admiralty chart drawn up following a 1830 survey,
with additions in 1845 and large corrections in 1864-65 and 1898. He compares the
differences in the names of some of the smaller cays, slight errors in latitude and
longitude, and changes in depth soundings.

Geology

35   **Geotectonic evolution and subsidence of Bahama Platform.**
Robert S. Dietz, John C. Holden, Walter P. Sproll. *Geological Society of America Bulletin*, vol. 81, no. 7 (July 1970), p. 1915-28.

In this highly scientific paper, the authors contend that the geological Bahamas, which includes the Turks and Caicos Islands, is part of Africa and the archipelago was formed by continental drift. This is a sound study of the geophysical evolution of the region.

36   **Sediments of the Caicos Outer Ridge, the Bahamas.**
Eric D. Schneider, Bruce C. Heezen. *Geological Society of America Bulletin*, vol. 77, no. 12 (Dec. 1966), p. 1381-98.

The Caicos Outer Ridge is an asymmetrical sedimentary ridge northeast of the Caicos Islands. Schneider and Heezen have determined that the ridge consists predominantly of clays deposited by a southeasterly flowing deep ocean current, also containing calcarenites which originated on the Bahama Banks and spread along the ridge and onto the surrounding abyssal plain.

37   **Bahamian platforms.**
Norman D. Newell. In: *Crust of the earth: a symposium*. Edited by Arie Poldervaart. New York: Geological Society of America, 1955, p. 303-15. (GSA Special Papers, no. 62).

Newell points out that the Bahamian platforms, which include the Turks and Caicos Islands, are among the best examples of contemporary limestone sea areas anywhere. In places, the pure carbonate deposits reach to a depth of 14,500 feet with no evidence of folding or faulting. These Bahamian platforms resemble Pacific coral atolls but are relatively new, having only been formed since the last glaciation. The author concludes that the platforms were formed by oolite deposits laid down over the original Tertiary reefs.

38 **Land forms of the Southeast Bahamas.**
Edwin Doran, Jr.   Austin, Texas: Department of Geography,
University of Texas, 1955. 38p. 12 maps. bibliog. (University of Texas
Publication, 5509).

This report describes and classifies the landforms of the southeast Bahamas, shows
their distribution on a series of maps at a scale of one inch per mile and comments on
their origin. Because the Turks and Caicos Islands are part of the Bahamas
geomorphically, they are included in Doran's report. There are sections on shallow
water forms, shoreline forms, plains forms, ridge forms and geomorphic history.

39 **Bahaman foreland and island festoon.**
Charles Schuchert.   In: *Historical geology of the Antillean-Caribbean*
region or the lands bordering the Gulf of Mexico and the Caribbean Sea.
Charles Schuchert. New York: Wiley; London: Chapman & Hall, 1935.
Reprinted, New York: Hafner, 1968, p. 528-50.

In this chapter, Schuchert discusses the Bahama foreland (i.e. submarine banks) and
the Bahama volcanic arc which includes the Turks and Caicos Islands. He also provides
information on the geological history of the area and notes on the flora and fauna.
Included is an extensive bibliography.

40 **The general characters and geological structure of the Turks Islands.**
Henry Brougham Guppy.   In: *Plants, seeds, and currents in the West*
Indies and Azores. Henry Brougham Guppy. London: Williams &
Norgate, 1917, p. 254-76.

Guppy outlines the general geological history of the Turks Islands as well as changes in
the levels of the islands, reclamations of land from the sea, the composite structure of
the larger islands and the probable destruction in great part of the original islands in
the Turks Islands group. There is also some additional information related to this
article in the appendix (note 39, p. 502-04). Guppy makes no mention of the Caicos
Islands in the article.

41 **Preliminary remarks on the geology of the Bahamas, with special**
reference to the origin of the Bahaman and Floridian oolites.
Thomas Wayland Vaughan.   *Publication of the Carnegie Institute of*
Washington, vol. 182 (1914), p. 47-54.

Vaughan examines the whole of the Bahamas in this article and includes the Turks and
Caicos Islands in his discussions. As well as outlining the activities of early geologists
and the results of their investigations from 1851 onwards, he examines both the
formation of Bahamian and Floridian oolites and the geologic history of the Bahamian
archipelago.

42 Physiography and geology of the Bahama Islands.

George Burbank Shattuck, Benjamin LeRoy Miller.   In:*The Bahama Islands*. George Burbank Shattuck. New York: Macmillan, 1905. p. 3-20.

Although very little mention is made of the Turks and Caicos Islands in this chapter, geologically, they are an intrinsic part of the Bahama Island chain. Shattuck and Miller discuss previous geologic investigations from 1853 to 1903 and comment extensively on the physiographic and geological features of the region as well as the area's topographic history.

43 A reconnoissance of the Bahamas and of the elevated reefs of Cuba, in the steam-yacht 'Wild Duck': January to April 1893.

Alexander Agassiz.   *Bulletin of the Museum of Comparative Zoology at Harvard College*, vol. 26, no. 1 (1894), p. 1-203.

This detailed examination of the geology of the Bahamas also includes the Turks and Caicos Islands. Following the 203 pages of text there are forty-seven plates which include eight charts, six soundings graphs and thirty-three photographs.

44 On the geology of the Bahamas and on coral formations generally.

Richard J. Nelson.   *Quarterly Journal of the Geological Society of London*, vol. 9 (1853), p. 200-15.

This is an early, general investigation of the geology of the Bahamian archipelago. It is still useful, especially for historical purposes.

Travel Guides

45 Diving, snorkeling & visitor's guide to the Turks & Caicos Islands.
    Bob Gascoine.   Grand Turk: The Author, 1991. 94p. 13 maps.

This is a very useful little guide describing sixty-one dive sites throughout the Turks and Caicos Islands. The emphasis is on those sites which are easily accessible to the hotel-based visitor. The photographs have been chosen for their documentary quality in order to best illustrate the dive location and its surroundings. Gascoine also provides general information on the islands along with lists of national parks, hotels and guest homes, and dive operators. This guide is available from Aquanaut, P.O. Box 101, Grand Turk, Turks and Caicos Islands, British West Indies.

46 The Caribbean islands handbook, 1990-.
    Edited by Ben Box, Sarah Cameron.   Bath, England: Trade & Travel
    Publications; New York: Simon & Schuster, 1989-. annual.

This tourist guide is aimed at the independent traveller who wishes to explore all aspects of island life and culture. The editors include information on history and government, the economy, diving and marine life, beaches and water sports, and birds of the Turks and Caicos Islands. There are also descriptions of all the major islands and cays.

47 Fodor's great travel values: Caribbean.
    New York: Fodor's Travel Guides, 1988-. annual.

This guide was first published in 1979 as *Fodor's budget Caribbean*. In 1985, the title was changed to *Fodor's budget travel Caribbean* and then to the present title in 1988. It is published for the cost-conscious traveller, providing information on accommodation, dining, sightseeing, shopping and entertainment.

Travel Guides

48   **Idyll curiosity.**
Don Gillmor.   *Gentlemen's Quarterly*, vol. 58 (Oct. 1988), p. 360, 362-66.
Gillmor provides some brief historical background but primarily offers a general description of Grand Turk and Salt Cay.

49   **Undiscovered islands of the Caribbean.**
Burl Willes.   Santa Fe, New Mexico: John Muir Publications, 1988. 209p. 23 maps. (JMP Travel).
In his section on the Turks and Caicos Islands (p. 37-59), Willes offers information on accommodation, dining and sightseeing. This guide also includes information on the lesser known islands of the Bahamas, as well as Puerto Rico, the Leeward Islands, the French West Indies, the Grenadines, Venezuela, Belize and the West Caribbean.

50   **A bit about Provo, the 'just discovered' West Indian Island.**
Russell DeCoudres.   Providenciales: The Author, 1987. 5th ed. 87p. map.
In this book, written for the tourist as well as the resident, DeCoudres supplies a great deal of information on history and government, communications and transportation, health and education, hotels and restaurants. There is also a commercial directory. It is available from P.O. Box 52-6002, Miami, Florida, 33152.

51   **The Caribbean.**
Frank Bellamy.   Chester, Connecticut: Globe Pequot Press, 1987. 358p. 40 maps. (Cadogan Guides).
In this easy-to-read, concise guide, Bellamy provides information about the Lesser Antilles, the Greater Antilles, and the Bahama Islands. The Turks and Caicos Islands (p. 244-53) are included under the Greater Antilles. The author gives information about currency, climate, population and history. He also describes each island with information on accommodation and diving. This guide was originally published in 1979 as *Caribbean island hopping* (London: Gentry; New York: Hippocrene, 280p.).

52   **Diver's almanac: guide to the Bahamas and Caribbean.**
Edited by Stephen F. Guettermann.   Costa Mesa, California: HDL Communications; Medford, Oregon: Sports Almanacs, 1987. 202p. 26 maps.
This profusely illustrated and glossy book covers a wealth of material. For each island the editor furnishes historical and topographic data, information on land-based attractions, dive services, dive site descriptions and transportation information concerning how to get to and around the island. There are also articles on weather, diving equipment and education, and the medical and safety aspects of diving.

53   **At Club Med, two variations on a theme.**
Eleanor Foa Dienstag.   *New York Times* (Jan. 26, 1986), p. 21, 36.
This is a fascinating comparison between the more public Club Med Caravelle on Guadeloupe and the more isolated Club Med Turkoise on Providenciales. There is also useful information about the general Club Med experience.

54 **Fodor's Caribbean.**
New York: Fodor's Travel Guides, 1986-. annual.
This annual began publication in 1960 under the title *Fodor's guide to the Caribbean, Bahamas, and Bermuda*. The publication subsequently became *Fodor's Caribbean, Bahamas, and Bermuda* and then in 1980, *Fodor's Caribbean and the Bahamas*. In 1986 the title was changed to *Fodor's Caribbean* when the publishers began a separate publication for the Bahamas. This very useful guide gives a great deal of practical information concerning accommodation, dining and shopping. There is also historical and descriptive information about the islands.

55 **Birnbaum's Caribbean, Bermuda and the Bahamas.**
Edited by Stephen Birnbaum. Boston, Massachusetts: Houghton Mifflin, 1985-. annual. (A Stephen Birnbaum Travel Guide.)
Birnbaum's guide gives information on accommodation, dining and island activities. However, because the guide includes the whole of the Caribbean as well as the Bahamas and Bermuda, coverage of the Turks and Caicos Islands is limited.

56 **A cruising guide to the Caribbean and the Bahamas, including the north coast of South America, Central America and Yucatan.**
Jerrems C. Hart, William T. Stone. New York: Dodd, Mead, 1982.
rev. ed. 626p. 147 maps. bibliog.
Chapter six (p. 157-63) in this work pertains to cruising in the Turks and Caicos Islands. The text and charts provide sailing information for the waters surrounding the Caicos Bank, Providenciales and Pine Cay, Cockburn Harbour, Grand Turk, Salt Cay and Sand Cay.

57 **Fielding's Caribbean.**
Margaret Zellers. New York: Fielding Travel Books, 1981-. annual.
This publication includes an introduction to the Turks and Caicos Islands and information on medical facilities, currency, communications, accommodation and dining, sports and sites to see. Hotels are rated on a one-to-five star system. Like Stephen Birnbaum's guide (q.v.), coverage is limited because the book deals with the whole of the Caribbean.

58 **Turks and Caicos: the timeless islands.**
Barbara Currie Maguire. *Americas*, vol. 32, no. 1 (Jan. 1980), p. 20-24.
Following a brief history, Maguire provides a general descriptive, non-judgemental travel article about the island group.

59 **Caribbean islands of the unexpected.**
Barbara Currie Maguire. *Saturday Evening Post*, vol. 251 (Oct. 1979), p. 78-81.
Along with some fascinating historical anecdotes and a great deal of description, Maguire emphasizes the lack of what she calls 'the expected civilized frills of prepackaged paradises' (p. 79). She concludes that the islands are 'among the other tropical jewels of the Caribbean' (p. 81), a statement as true today as it was in 1979.

60 **Pilot's Bahamas aviation guide: including the Turks and Caicos Islands and Haiti.**
Dale Cady, edited by Kelly Dunigan, Donn Pfaff. Ocala, Florida: Pilot, 1979-. annual.

For each island, the editors provide a map, a description and photograph of, and the approach to each airstrip, as well as general remarks and information on climate, communications, accommodation and dining, medical services, customs procedures, fuel supplies and maintenance services.

61 **Paradise found?**
Ann Bolt. *West Indies Chronicle*, vol. 90, no. 1536 (1977), p. 14-15, 17.

Bolt looks at tourist facilities in the mid-1970s on Grand Turk, Salt Cay, Pine Cay, Providenciales and North and South Caicos. She also examines the Turks and Caicos Islands' potential for tourism and the problem of tourist growth destroying the peace and charm of the islands.

62 **Diving guide to the Bahamas: including Turks and Caicos Islands.**
Gordon Lomer. New York: Hastings House, 1975. 56p. 25 maps.

Lomer attempts to detail as many specific dive sites as possible and to give descriptive comments as to depths and features of each area. Although this slim volume is not as detailed as other diving guides, it does offer a useful overview for the first-time diver. It also includes 117 small colour photographs of marine life, for identification purposes.

63 **Have you ever heard of the Turks & Caicos Islands?**
J. Wandres. *Travel*, vol. 144 (Dec. 1975), p. 34-37, 67.

Wandres gives a brief history and description of the islands along with the accommodation to be found.

64 **Bahama Islands: a boatman's guide to the land and the water.**
J. Linton Rigg, revised by Harry Kline. New York: Scribner, 1973. 4th ed. 292p. 137 maps.

This is one of the first (1949) and most important sailing guides to the Bahamas and includes information on the Turks and Caicos Islands. Kline provides charts and directions for cruising throughout all the islands, but does indicate in his preface that the information is 'subject to change'. It is advisable to use the *Yachtsman's guide to the Bahamas* (q.v.) in conjunction with this text.

65 **Flight to paradise: tourist's guide to the Bahama Islands and Turks and Caicos Islands.**
Lloyd R. Wilson, James E. Landfried. Melbourne, Florida: Islands Unlimited, 1971. 172p. 18 maps.

In the section dealing with the Turks and Caicos Islands, the authors begin with a short introduction and history and follow this up with information on accommodation and activities on four of the major islands (Grand Turk, Providenciales, Salt Cay and South Caicos Island). There is also a section outlining future proposed developments.

66 **Bahamian backyard.**
Pete Petersen. *Travel*, vol. 108 (Dec. 1957), p. 55-58.
This is an idyllic description of South Caicos and an examination of the then thriving salt industry only a few years before its collapse.

67 **Caicos cruise.**
Edwin Beal Doran. *Motor Boating*, (Dec. 1957), p. 28-29, 63-64, 66, 68, 70.
Doran describes various of the islands in the Turks and Caicos group and extols the delights of cruising through this region. He comments particularly on the island harbours and passages.

68 **Yachtsman's guide to the Bahamas.**
Edited by Meredith Helleberg Fields. Miami, Florida: Tropic Isle, 1950-. annual.
The *Yachtsman's guide* gives a thorough description of the waters, reefs and shallows near virtually every island and cay in the Bahamas and the Turks and Caicos Islands. It also includes information on communications and safety, the documents required for official entry and coastal inspections. Veteran yachtsmen deem this guide to be indispensable to people sailing these waters in a yacht.

69 **Fishing guide to the Bahamas: including Turks and Caicos Islands.**
George W. Hartwell. Miami, Florida: Argos; New York: Hastings House, [n.d.]. 64p. 14 maps.
Hartwell has written a guide to the types of gamefish in the waters of the Bahamas and the Turks and Caicos Islands as well as to where these fish may be found. For each island he discusses, Hartwell provides a map showing where certain gamefish can usually be spotted and gives general information and tips, as well as information on gamefish records.

Travellers' Accounts

70 **Turks & Caicos Islands.**
Arlene Alexandrovich. *Great Expeditions*, no. 29 (Oct./Nov. 1983),
p. 6-11.
This article is just as much a travel guide as it is an account of Alexandrovich's stay in the islands. There are descriptions of all of the inhabited islands with comments on dive sites, sightseeing and accommodation. Most of the author's time was spent on Middle Caicos and she provides a diary of her stay there.

71 **Up and down the cays.**
Graham Norton. *West Indies Chronicle*, vol. 90, no. 1523 (Dec. 1974/
Jan. 1975), p. 6-9.
Norton's article is described by the editors as 'a perceptive, realistic and amusing account of a recent visit to the Turks and Caicos Islands'. He provides descriptions of all the major islands and concludes that tourism remains the only hope for their future.

72 **Salt and sermons.**
Peter Bleackley. *Corona*, vol. 14 (Dec. 1962), p. 461-64.
This is a fond recollection of life in the Turks and Caicos Islands in the 1950s written by a member of the Colonial Office for other members of the Civil Service. Interestingly, Bleackley states matter-of-factly and without providing any scholarly proof that Columbus did indeed first land in the Turks and Caicos Islands.

73 **The voyage of the 'Priscilla', by the mate.**
J.C. Crisson. Bermuda: Colonist, 1907. 53p.
This is a delightful, descriptive memoir of a return voyage between Bermuda and the Turks and Caicos Islands around the turn of the century. The outward voyage (p. 1-16) and the homeward voyage (p. 41-52) are based on the ship's log; while the descriptions of the time spent in the islands (p. 17-40) are based on Crisson's own observations and

exploits. The *Priscilla* was delivering lumber to the islands and returning with salt so that a great deal of Crisson's description is of the salt industry.

74 **A visit to Turks Islands.**
   Thomas Capper. *Journal of the Institute of Jamaica*, vol. 2 (1895), p. 120-30.

Capper spent three weeks in the Turks and Caicos Islands as Inspector of Schools, travelling from Jamaica to report on the condition of schools at the request of the commissioner of the Turks Islands. In this article, he provides general descriptions of Grand Turk, Salt Cay, East Caicos, North Caicos and Grand Caicos. He also comments on geology, geography, vegetation and the salt industry. Curiously, there is no discussion of the schools or education.

75 **Notes on 'A governor's cruise in the West Indies in 1884': being an abridgement of a narrative written by Sir H.W. Norman.**
   J.P. Thomson. *Quarterly of the Royal Geographical Society of Australia*, vol. 9 (1894), p. 7-14.

This article outlines Sir Henry W. Norman's cruise in 1884. At the time, he was governor of Jamaica and, as governor, was also responsible for the Cayman Islands and the Turks and Caicos Islands. Along with a brief history of the Cayman Islands, there is information about the Turks and Caicos' population, imports and exports, and government as well as a very good description of Grand Turk.

76 **Stark's history and guide to the Bahama Islands, containing a description of everything on or about the Bahama Islands of which the visitor or resident may desire information, including their history, inhabitants, climate, agriculture, geology, government and resources.**
   James Henry Stark. Boston, Massachusetts: Plimpton, 1891. 243p. 5 maps.

Stark's work is a combined history and travel account. Although it is devoted primarily to the Bahamas, some mention is made of the Turks and Caicos Islands since many nineteenth-century and early twentieth-century travellers saw the two island groups as one country. Stark includes information on slavery, government, agriculture, sponging, geology, climate, religion and education.

77 **A summer on the borders of the Caribbean Sea.**
   J. Dennis Harris. New York: Burdick, 1890; Negro Universities Press, 1969. 179p.

This is an account of Harris's travels in the summer of 1860. Harris, a free coloured American, visited the Dominican Republic, Haiti, the Turks and Caicos Islands, and British Honduras with the purpose of investigating the possibility of establishing colonies in and around the Gulf of Mexico for coloured people under the protection of the United States government. He concluded that either Haiti or the Dominican Republic offered the most promising prospects. Harris discusses the Turks and Caicos Islands in Letter (i.e. chapter) XIV, p. 128-37, under the heading, 'Grand Turk's [sic] and Caicos Islands'.

Tourism

78 **Turks and Caicos Islands: tourism development plan: final report.**
Great Britain. Overseas Development Administration. London:
Coopers & Lybrand Associates, 1986. 280p. 14 maps. bibliog.
This extensive report is designed to spur tourist development throughout the islands
with discussions of resources and opportunities, constraints and potential, strategies
and design concepts, social and economic implications, and promotion and marketing.
The main recommendations include a call for: marketing consultants and a stronger
Tourism Office; improvements to the islands' infrastructure; educational improve-
ments; and improved inter-island transportation.

79 **Social cost-benefit analysis and the appraisal of tourism projects in a
developing island economy.**
W. Angus Laidlaw. MA thesis, Carleton University, Ottawa, 1981.
(Available from National Library of Canada, Ottawa, Ontario, order
no. 52793).
Laidlaw focuses on the roots, uses and limitations of cost-benefit analysis and suggests
that it could be used to determine the social profitability of alternative proposals for
involvement in tourism in a small island economy. He uses the Turks and Caicos
Islands as a basis for this study, presenting a good overview of the history, geography
and economy of the islands with a detailed discussion of tourism in the islands from
1960 to 1980.

80 **Turks and Caicos: orderly tourist growth.**
John H. Lang. *Canadian Commerce*, vol. 137, no. 1 (Jan. 1973), p. 7-
8.
In an update to Leavitt's 1970 article (q.v.), Lang outlines plans for further tourist
growth and opportunities for Canadian businesspeople.

81 **Property and tourist development in the Turks and Caicos Islands.**
Derek Jakeway.   London: Foreign and Commonwealth Office, 1970.
[n.p.]. map.
This report was produced by a seven-member working party, under the chairmanship
of Sir Derek Jakeway, which was sent to the Turks and Caicos Islands to examine the
future growth of property and tourist development. The report provides background
information and a look at contemporary conditions and views on development. It
outlines the implications of future growth on budgetary/financial matters and social/
political conditions. The report also includes the committee's conclusions and
recommendations: an expansion of the islands' infrastructure and social services,
particularly education; increased construction on Providenciales; the establishment of a
development unit in the Turks and Caicos government; the reorganization of the
educational system; and the establishment of a development corporation. There are
also appendices detailing development projects, possible tax guarantees, government
staffing needs, and education.

82 **White sands and coral reefs.**
Donald H. Leavitt.   *Foreign Trade*, vol. 134, no. 8 (Nov. 21, 1970),
p. 20-22.
Leavitt outlines tourism development and the tourist situation in the late 1960s in the
Turks and Caicos Islands, with a discussion of the future development and the
opportunities for Canadian businessmen and investors.

Flora and Fauna

General

83   **A field guide to southeastern and Caribbean seashores: Cape Hatteras to the Gulf Coast, Florida, and the Caribbean.**
Eugene Herbert Kaplan.   Boston, Massachusetts: Houghton Mifflin, 1988. 425p. map. bibliog. (Peterson Field Guide Series, 36).

This work, sponsored by the National Audubon Society and the National Wildlife Federation, describes the ecology and common organisms of seashores from North Carolina through to Florida, the Gulf of Mexico Coast and the Caribbean. Kaplan identifies plants and animals and describes the various types of seashore environments – sandy beaches, rocky shores, turtle grass beds, mangrove swamps and scrub forests. A glossary is included.

84   **The natural world of the Turks and Caicos Islands.**
Katherine Shelley Orr, Jane Allison Halaby.   Rockville, Maryland: McCollum, 1983. 62p.

This children's picture book, for seven to ten-year-olds, discusses geology, botany, zoology, the seashore and marine life. Although written primarily for Turks and Caicos children, it would also be of interest to children elsewhere.

85   **The ephemeral islands: a natural history of the Bahamas.**
David G. Campbell.   London: Macmillan, 1978. 151p. 2 maps. bibliog.

Campbell includes the Turks and Caicos Islands with the southeastern islands of the Bahamian archipelago (Crooked, Acklins and Mayaguana Islands) in his examination of the geological, evolutionary and historical processes which combined to form these island groups. He also discusses birds, coral, fishes, crustaceans, flora, gastropods, insects, mammals, reptiles and spiders. The work is easy to read and understand as Campbell avoids technical jargon.

86 **Report on the botanical exploration of the Bahama and Caicos Islands.**
Marshall A. Howe, Percy Wilson. *Journal of the New York Botanical Garden*, vol. 9, no. 99 (March 1908), p. 41-50.

The object of this visit, undertaken between November 1907 and January 1908, was to collect herbarium and museum specimens illustrating both land and marine flora. This is Howe and Wilson's description of some of the more interesting specimens found during their expedition to the eastern and southeastern Bahama Islands and the Caicos Islands. In the Caicos Islands group, expedition members visited Fort George Cay, Pine Cay, Providenciales, as well as North, South and West Caicos. Over 8,000 specimens were collected.

87 **Turks Island and the guano caves of the Caicos Islands.**
S.P. Sharples. *Proceedings of the Boston Society of Natural History*, vol. 22 (1883), p. 242-52.

Sharples describes a visit to the guano caves on Cape Comet, twenty miles west of Grand Turk Island. Based on studies of the guano composition, he concludes that the caves contain fossil rather than fresh guano. There is also a brief description of Grand Turk Island and the salt industry.

Vegetation

88 **Fruits and vegetables of the Caribbean.**
M.J. Bourne, G.W. Lennox, S.A. Seddon. London: Macmillan Caribbean, 1988. 58p.

This handy, illustrated guide identifies forty-eight of the most commonly found fruits and vegetables of the region, including the Turks and Caicos Islands. The authors have described each species' origin, its botanical characteristics and its uses.

89 **Caribbean wild plants and their uses.**
Penelope N. Honychurch. London: Macmillan Caribbean, 1986. 166p. bibliog.

Honychurch describes and illustrates close to one hundred wild plants in the Caribbean (including the Turks and Caicos Islands) which are used as remedies for illness or have folklore associations. The main body of the book contains detailed information on seventy-three dicotyledons (plants having two seed leaves), twenty monocotyledons (plants having one seed leaf) and five miscellaneous plants. There are also lists of medicinal compounds and the plants in which they are found, and a list of the plants classified under the ailments for which they were or may be used as the remedy. A glossary provides a list of botanical terms and there are indexes of French and patois names, English names and scientific names.

90 **Flora of the Bahamian archipelago (including the Turks and Caicos Islands).**
Donovan S. Correll, Helen B. Correll. Vaduz: J. Cramer, 1982. 1692p. map. bibliog.

This work provides a means for the identification of the indigenous and naturalized flowering plants and ferns in the Bahamian archipelago. The flora are divided into four sections: ferns, flowering plants, grasses and palms, and trees. The families are arranged phylogenetically while the genera and species are arranged alphabetically. The entries are well-written and very thorough. However, given its large size, this guide cannot be used easily in the field. The work includes a glossary and 715 illustrations.

91 **Trees of the Caribbean.**
S.A. Seddon, G.W. Lennox. London: Macmillan Caribbean, 1980. 74p.

This guide has been designed as a companion to *Flowers of the Caribbean* (q.v.) and, as such, is for individuals with little or no botanical training. The trees are divided into four sections: ornamental trees, fruit trees, coast trees, and palm and palm-like trees. For each entry, the authors have provided at least one colour photograph; information regarding leaf shape, size and colour; and descriptions of the flower and fruit. Each entry also includes the botanical family name and the scientific and common names for each species.

92 **Flowers of the Caribbean, the Bahamas, and Bermuda.**
G.W. Lennox, S.A. Seddon. London: Macmillan, 1978. 72p.

This book is designed for individuals with little or no botanical background. The flora are divided into three sections: herbs and shrubs, trees, and orchids. For each of the fifty entries, the authors have provided a colour photograph; the common, local and scientific names; and a short description of the specimen. Although this handy guide does not cover all species of flowering plants, it does discuss the more common ones.

93 **Flowers of the West Indies: Caribbean and Bahamas.**
Hans W. Hannau, Jeanne Garrard. Miami, Florida: Argos, 1970. 63p.

An introductory text is followed by thirty-four colour plates, each with its own descriptive caption, although the captions do not appear immediately beside the illustrations. This is a small picture book rather than a field guide or scientific treatise, and the emphasis on high quality colour plates is typical of Hannau's books.

94 **Comparative variability and relationships of Caribbean pine (*Pinus caribaea*, Mor.) and slash pine (*Pinus elliottii*, Engelm).**
Donald Garth Nikles. PhD thesis, North Carolina State University, Raleigh, North Carolina, 1967. (Available from University Microfilms, Ann Arbor, Michigan, order no. 67-15695).

Nikles examined cone, seed, foliage and wood samples from 260 Caribbean pines in thirteen areas throughout the Bahamas and the Caicos Islands. He also conducted similar studies on slash pines from the eastern coast of Florida. He concluded that Caicos Islands pines are different from Bahamas pines due to environmental selection reinforced by isolation and possible genetic drift. Much of his attention is given to

Pinus caribaea var. *bahamensis* because it has the greatest potential for reforestation in the subtropics and may be the intermediate between the two species, *Pinus caribaea* and *Pinus elliottii.*

95 **Tropical trees found in the Caribbean, South America, Central America, Mexico.**
Dorothy Hargreaves, Bob Hargreaves.   Portland, Oregon: Hargreaves Industrial, 1965. 64p.
This booklet provides a descriptive annotation and colour photograph for seventy trees found throughout the region. Each annotation gives a good description; a note on geographic distribution; and the scientific name in Latin, as well as the common name in English, Spanish, French and Dutch.

96 **Tropical blossoms of the Caribbean.**
Dorothy Hargreaves, Bob Hargreaves.   Lahaina, Hawaii: Ross-Hargreaves, 1960. 64p.
This handbook includes entries for both flowers and trees from the Caribbean region and tropical South America. Each entry is accompanied by a colour photograph and includes the common and botanical names, as well as a description and a location. It is similar in format to the authors' *Tropical trees. . .*(q.v.).

97 **Notes on the vegetation of the Turks and Caicos Islands.**
George R. Proctor.   *Natural History Notes of the Natural History Society of Jamaica,* vol. 70 (1955), p. 149-52, 170-74, 199-203.
In this three-part series, Proctor discusses previous expeditions and collections and outlines species of trees, ferns, shrubs and cacti found on Grand Turk (part I); South Caicos (part II); and North, Middle and East Caicos and Providenciales (part III).

98 **The Bahama flora.**
Nathaniel Lord Britton, Charles Frederick Millspaugh.   New York: The Authors, 1920; New York: Hafner, 1962. 695p. bibliog.
This highly scientific ordering of Bahamian flora contains over 1,900 species that fall under the phyla of Spermatophyta, Pteridophyta, Bryophyta and Thallophyta as well as a list of explorations and collections of Bahamian flora from 1703 to 1911. The detailed descriptions for each species include locations; a majority are found throughout the Turks and Caicos Islands. There are no illustrations. It is a work for the scientist or well-informed layperson.

99 **The flora of the Turks Islands.**
Henry Brougham Guppy.   In: *Plants, seeds, and currents in the West Indies and Azores.* Henry Brougham Guppy. London: Williams & Norgate, 1917, p. 277-93.
Guppy discusses the sparse scrub vegetation on the smaller islands of the Turks Islands group but provides more detail concerning the plants found on Grand Turk. He also provides a list of plants found on the islands and offers some suggestions on how they were spread – by currents, birds, floating logs or man.

100   **Grasses of the West Indies.**
      A.S. Hitchcock, Agnes Chase.   *Contributions from the United States
      National Herbarium,* vol. 18 (Sept. 1, 1917), p. 261-471.

This is a detailed list of the grasses, many found in the Turks and Caicos Islands, from
over one hundred genera. Each entry includes the scientific and common names; a
description; and an indication of location and distribution. The list is based primarily
on a study of the collection in the United States National Herbarium. Also included is
a sixty-seven-page catalogue of the National Herbarium collection arranged by
collectors' names and National Herbarium numbers.

101   **The larger foreign drift of the Turks Islands.**
      Henry Brougham Guppy.   In: *Plants, seeds, and currents in the West
      Indies and Azores.* Henry Brougham Guppy. London: Williams &
      Norgate, 1917, p. 111-65.

Guppy provides information about those plants which have reached the Turks Islands
by ocean currents, discussing and describing twenty-four species in detail.

102   **Provisional list of the plants of the Bahama Islands.**
      John Gardiner, L.J.K. Brace, Charles S. Dolley.   *Proceedings of the
      Academy of Natural Sciences of Philadelphia,* vol. 41 (1889), p. 349-
      407.

This list of plants from both the Bahamas and the Turks and Caicos Islands includes
115 families, 410 genera and 621 species.

103   **Flora of the British West Indian Islands.**
      August Heinrich Rudolf Grisebach.   London: Lovell Reeve, 1864.
      789p.

Grisebach's work is a descriptive list of more than 3,400 species of flora found
throughout the Caribbean, including the Bahamas and the Turks and Caicos Islands.
For each species, he gives a description, the scientific name and a location. However,
there are no illustrations.

Marine life

104   **JoJo: rogue dolphin?**
      Doug Perrine.   *Sea Frontiers,* vol. 36, no. 2 (March/April 1990), p. 32-
      41.

JoJo is a male Atlantic bottlenose dolphin which first appeared off the Island of
Providenciales in 1984 when the Club Med Turkoise opened. He alternately attacked
and played with swimmers, and in 1988, dolphin experts began studying JoJo. These
initial studies led to the JoJo Dolphin Project sponsored by the Society for the
Protection of Reefs and Islands from Degradation and Exploitation (PRIDE), a

conservation foundation. This article describes the JoJo Project and speculates on the causes of JoJo's behaviour.

105   **Guide to the marine isopod crustaceans of the Caribbean.**
     Brian Kensley, Marilyn Schotte.   Washington, DC: Smithsonian Institution Press, 1989. 308p. 3 maps. bibliog.
In the main body of this guide, Kensley and Schotte discuss the eight suborders of Order Isopoda. The families, genera and species are all presented alphabetically and a record of where each species can be found throughout the Caribbean region, including the Turks and Caicos Islands, is given. There is also a short introduction to Order Isopoda and a glossary.

106   **Marine plants of the Caribbean: a field guide from Florida to Brazil.**
     Diane Scullion Littler, Mark M. Littler, Katina E. Bucher, James N. Norris.   Washington, DC: Smithsonian Institution Press, 1989. 263p. map. bibliog.
This work describes 204 species of algae and five species of seagrasses which represent the common species most likely to be encountered in the waters of the Caribbean. Each entry provides a brief description giving size, shape, colour, depth and habitat along with a colour photograph. Technical terms are kept to a minimum but a glossary has been appended. This guide is very useful for quick identification.

107   **A field guide to coral reefs of the Caribbean and Florida: a guide to the common invertebrates and fishes of Bermuda, the Bahamas, southern Florida, the West Indies, and the Caribbean coast of Central and South America.**
     Eugene Herbert Kaplan.   Boston, Massachusetts: Houghton Mifflin, 1982. 289p. map. bibliog. (Peterson Field Guide Series, 27).
Following a very good introductory chapter, Kaplan provides an overview of coral reefs, their development and their ecology. The bulk of the work is devoted to the animals of the lagoon and the reef. Technical terms are kept to a minimum as the book is intended for laypeople, though a glossary is provided. The work is illustrated by thirty-seven colour plates and sponsored by the National Audubon Society and the National Wildlife Federation.

108   **Handguide to the coral reef fishes of the Caribbean and adjacent tropical waters including Florida, Bermuda and the Bahamas.**
     F. Joseph Stokes.   New York: Lippincott & Crowell, 1980. 160p.
The emphasis in this guide is on the illustrations, which are paintings of colour photographs, while the descriptions in the text often consist of only one sentence or several short phrases. The 460 species described are the ones most likely to be seen by the snorkeler and diver. This book, which includes a glossary, is useful for both professionals and amateurs.

109 **Seashore life of Florida and the Caribbean: a guide to the common marine invertebrates and plants of the Atlantic from Bermuda and the Bahamas to the West Indies and the Gulf of Mexico.**
Gilbert L. Voss.   Miami, Florida: Banyan, 1980. rev. ed. 199p. map. bibliog.

The species which Voss includes in this guide represent only a small part of the total fauna: those that one might reasonably expect to find down to a depth of fifty feet. Nevertheless, this book includes a great many species from thirteen invertebrate phyla (sponges, jellyfish, corals, sea anemones, sea fans, flatworms, ribbon worms, sea slugs, squids, crustaceans, sea stars, sea urchins and sea cucumbers) and four plant phyla (algae and sea grasses). Each entry is written in simple language and there are also 400 drawings and 19 very good colour photographs.

110 **Fishes of the Caribbean reefs, the Bahamas and Bermuda.**
Ian F. Took.   London: Macmillan, 1979. 92p. map.

Took's work is an introduction to some of the more common and spectacular fish to be found around the Caribbean and tropical west Atlantic reefs. For each of the eighty-five species covered, he provides a description, including length, common and scientific names; a discussion of general habits and particular characteristics; and an indication of where the fish might be found. There are also sections on practical fish watching, underwater photography and conservation of the coral reef. The work is illustrated with seventy-two colour plates of fish and seven of coral.

111 **Marine life of the Caribbean.**
Alick Jones, Nancy Sefton.   London: Macmillan Caribbean, 1979.
90p. map. bibliog.

This work, which is suitable as a school text for twelve to sixteen-year-olds, provides ecological information on mangroves; sandy shore and rocky shore areas; sea grass beds and coral reefs; and the open sea. There is also a chapter on sea turtles and the ecology and conservation of the Caribbean area. The book is heavily illustrated with black-and-white photographs and ink drawings though some colour photographs are also included. The authors have also provided a short glossary.

112 **Movement and migration of the queen conch, *Strombus gigas*, in the Turks and Caicos Islands.**
Katherine O. Hesse.   *Bulletin of Marine Science*, vol. 29, no. 3 (July 1979), p. 303-11.

From March 1974 to October 1975, the author studied a population of more than ten thousand queen conches at Six Hill Cays in the Turks and Caicos Islands. This study provided information on the growth and movement of conches and suggested the existence of migratory behaviour of a seasonal nature. Hesse's article describes the study site, the survey methods employed, the results of the study, and her conclusions.

113 **Caribbean reef invertebrates and plants: a field guide to the invertebrates and plants occurring on coral reefs of the Caribbean, the Bahamas and Florida.**
Patrick Lynn Colin. Hong Kong: T.F.H. Publications, 1978. 512p. map. bibliog.

This book is designed to serve as an identification guide for the professional marine scientist and the amateur snorkeler or scuba diver. Colin provides good introductory chapters on the natural history of Caribbean reefs and their organisms. The entries are arranged by phylum, with animals preceding plants. Within each phylum, the individual species are considered by order and family. Descriptions given for each entry are very good, while the black-and-white and colour photographs are adequate. Sponges, sea fans and sea anemones, corals, marine worms, crustaceans, molluscs, starfish, sea urchins and sea cucumbers, and marine plants and algae are all included. This work can easily be used as a companion to Randall's *Caribbean reef fishes* (q.v.).

114 **Waterproof guide to corals and fishes of Florida, the Bahamas and the Caribbean.**
Idaz Greenberg, Jerry Greenberg. Miami, Florida: Seahawk, 1977. 64p.

This booklet contains colour drawings and short descriptions for 206 fish and amphibians, fifty-three corals and eleven dangerous corals and fish, such as jellyfish, stinging corals, sea urchins and electric rays.

115 **The many-splendored fishes of the Atlantic coast including the fishes of the Gulf of Mexico, Florida, Bermuda, the Bahamas and the Caribbean.**
Gar Goodson. Palos Verdes Estates, California: Marquest Colorguide, 1976. 204p. 2 maps.

For each of the 408 entries, Goodson provides both the common name and the scientific name, a description, a distribution range and an indication as to whether it is edible. Though not as complete as Kaplan's *A field guide to coral reefs . . .* (q.v.) in terms of textual material, this volume is more useful than Stokes' *Handguide to the coral reef fishes . . .* (q.v.).

116 **Seashells of the West Indies: a guide to marine molluscs of the Caribbean.**
Michael Humfrey. New York: Taplinger, 1975. 351p. map. bibliog. (Taplinger World Wide Field Guides).

This guide, written primarily for the beginner seashell collector but also useful for the professional or experienced amateur, is designed to achieve four purposes: to provide a general illustrated guide to West Indian marine shells; to examine the habitat of each of the 497 shells described and illustrated; to provide a census of all known Jamaican marine molluscs; and to examine in detail the most efficient methods of collecting, cleaning and storing shells. Each entry lists the scientific and popular names, and the range, description and occurrence of the species. There is also a good introductory section in which Humfrey discusses mollusc classification and structure, environment, feeding and breeding habits, identification and distribution.

117 **Tropical marine fishes of southern Florida and the Bahama Islands.**
Warren Zeiller.   South Brunswick, New Jersey: A.S. Barnes, 1975.
125p. bibliog.

The bulk of this work consists of 289 colour plates with brief descriptions for each species. Accurate and accessible, it is useful for the student of tropical fish as well as the tropical fish fancier.

118 **In the coral reefs of the Caribbean, Bahamas, Florida, Bermuda.**
Hans W. Hannau.   Garden City, New York: Doubleday, 1974. 135p.

This general introduction to coral reefs is accompanied by ninety-four colour plates. Each chapter is by a different contributor which does lead to a patchy quality, and to over-simplified material being combined with highly technical information. There are useful chapters on corals, molluscs, fish and reef ecology but this picture-book for the 'armchair' explorer would be improved by maps and an index.

119 **Tropical marine invertebrates of southern Florida and the Bahama Islands.**
Warren Zeiller.   New York: Wiley, 1974. 132p. bibliog. (A Wiley-Interscience Publication).

Zeiller provides descriptions of examples of six of the twenty-seven invertebrate phyla: Coelenterata (polyp animals), Platyhelminthes (flatworms), Mollusca (molluscs), Annelida (segmented worms), Arthropoda (arthropods) and Echinodermata (echinoderms). For each of the 183 examples, he gives the phylum, class, order and family; the common and scientific names; the etymology of the scientific name; a short description; and a colour photograph. Zeiller includes an appendix in which all the specimens are listed in phyletic sequence, from primitive to more specialized life forms. The work does not include plant life, microfauna or sponges.

120 **Beneath the seas of the West Indies: Caribbean, Bahamas, Florida, Bermuda.**
Hans W. Hannau, Bernd H. Mock.   New York: Hastings House, 1973. 104p.

The authors discuss reefs and reef ecology and marine archaeology in the West Indies. The book includes fifty-four large colour plates and 120 small colour plates, as well as a picture portfolio for the identification of exotic, tropical fish which inhabit reef areas.

121 **The living reef: corals and fishes of Florida, the Bahamas, Bermuda and the Caribbean.**
Jerry Greenberg, Idaz Greenberg.   Miami, Florida: Seahawk, 1972. 110p.

This work consists chiefly of excellent underwater colour photographs. Although none of the locations of the photographs is identified, they are all typical of coral reefs found throughout the Caribbean.

122   **Caribbean reef fishes.**
John E. Randall.   Jersey City, New Jersey: T.F.H. Publications, 1968.
318p.

Randall's primary purpose is to provide identification of the 300 most common fishes
that might be observed while snorkeling or diving on the reefs of the Caribbean Sea.
The species examined are arranged in approximate phylogenetic sequence beginning
with cartilaginous fishes, i.e. sharks and rays. For each fish discussed, Randall gives an
illustration, the common and scientific names, the length and description, and an
indication of location. Most illustrations are black-and-white; colour plates are limited.
There is also a glossary of ichthyological terms.

123   **Fishes of the Bahamas and adjacent tropical waters.**
James E. Bohlke, Charles C.G. Chaplin.   Wynnewood, Pennsylvania:
Livingston, 1968. 771p. 2 maps. bibliog.

This excellent book lists approximately 700 species of fish found in the waters of the
Bahamas and the Turks and Caicos Islands. Each entry includes size, distinctions,
colouring and distribution, and general remarks. There is also an introduction which
includes a history of the study of the fish of this area, as well as a glossary and thirty-six
colour plates. This work is very complete but, because of its size, it cannot easily be
used in the field.

124   **Caribbean seashells: a guide to the marine mollusks of Puerto Rico and
other West Indian Islands, Bermuda and the lower Florida Keys.**
Germaine Le Clerc Warmke, R. Tucker Abbott.   Norberth,
Pennsylvania: Livingston, 1961. 348p. 21 maps. bibliog.

Although the emphasis in this work is on the seashells found in the waters off Puerto
Rico, the authors have included the Turks and Caicos Islands along with other West
Indian islands. Warmke and Abbott provide information on periwinkles, conches and
other snails (Class Gastropoda), scallops, oysters and other clams (Class Pelecypoda),
and squids, chitons and tusk shells (Classes Cephalopoda, Amphineura and Scaphopoda).
There are thirty-four black-and-white drawings in the text along with four colour and
forty black-and-white plates. Entries include a description and distribution range as
well as the scientific and common names of each specimen.

125   **Deepsea Berycomorphi and Percomorphi from the waters around the
Bahama and Bermuda Islands.**
Albert Eide Parr.   *Bulletin of the Bingham Oceanographic Collection*,
vol. 3, no. 6 (Dec. 1933), p. 1-51.

Parr provides detailed descriptions and drawings of twenty-nine species including two
newly discovered families, six new genera and eleven new species. Eight of the species
described come from the Turks and Caicos Islands.

126   Teleostean shore and shallow-water fishes from the Bahamas and Turks
      Island.
      Albert Eide Parr.   *Bulletin of the Bingham Oceanographic Collection*,
      vol. 3, no. 4 (July 1930), p. 1-148.
This is Parr's report on 150 species of teleostean shore and shallow-water fishes
gathered as a result of the third oceanographic expedition of the *Pawnee* in 1927. The
species are described in great detail, especially the Atlantic eels of the genus *Myrophis*,
the western Atlantic flying fishes of the genus *Cypselurus*, damselfishes, razor fishes
and parrot fishes of the genus *Pseudoscarus*.

127   Deepsea fishes of the Order Iniomi from the waters around the Bahama
      and Bermuda Islands.
      Alberta Eide Parr.   *Bulletin of the Bingham Oceanographic Collection*,
      vol. 3, no. 3 (Dec. 1928), p. 1-193.
Parr offers detailed descriptions and some drawings of species taken from fifty-three
monitoring stations, eight of which are situated around the Turks and Caicos Islands.
Examples of seventeen species under investigation were taken off the Turks and Caicos
Islands.

128   A list of Turk Islands fishes, with a description of a new flatfish.
      John Treadwell Nichols.   *Bulletin of the American Museum of
      Natural History*, vol. 44 (1921), p. 21-24.
Nichols' 1921 description of a newly discovered species of flatfish found in the waters
off the Turks and Caicos Islands is accompanied by a list of 166 species of fishes found
in the same waters. The fish listed were originally collected by Louis L. Mowbray in
1916.

129   Fishes of the Bahama Islands.
      Barton A. Bean.   In: *The Bahama Islands*. George Burbank Shattuck.
      New York: Macmillan, 1905, p. 293-325.
Barton lists annotations for 183 species of fishes found in the waters surrounding the
Bahama Islands and the Turks and Caicos Islands. This chapter includes five colour
plates with another five found elsewhere in the volume.

Birds

130   The birds of the southern Bahamas: an annotated check-list.
      Donald W. Buden.   London: British Ornithologists' Union, 1987.
      119p. 3 maps. bibliog. (British Ornithologists' Union. Series of
      Checklists, no. 8).
Based largely on the author's 1979 PhD dissertation from Louisiana State University,
this work covers the major islands of the southern Bahamas as well as all the islands of
the Turks and Caicos archipelago. An introductory chapter provides material on

geography and geology, palaeontology, climate, vegetation and previous ornithological explorations. The bulk of the book consists of a systematic list of 183 species giving information on breeding habits and location of the species along with individual descriptions and other observations. This is a book for the specialist rather than the weekend bird watcher. There are no illustrations.

131 **New subspecies of Thick-billed Vireo (Aves: Vireonidae) from the Caicos Islands, with remarks on taxonomic status of the other populations.**
Donald W. Buden. *Proceedings of the Biological Society of Washington*, vol. 98, no. 3 (August 30, 1985), p. 591-97.
Vireo crassirostris stalagmium is described as a new subspecies of vireo from the Caicos Islands and is compared with other subspecies.

132 **Birds of the Turks and Caicos Islands.**
David J. Sanderson. *Turks & Caicos Current*, vol. 1, no. 9 (Nov./ Dec. 1982), p. 35-42.
Sanderson lists 184 species found throughout the islands. Each entry includes the common and scientific names plus comments on the status of each species (i.e. is the species common, uncommon, rare, etc.). Sanderson also provides a commentary on the legal status of birds in the islands and an indication of the best bird watching localities.

133 **Birds of the Bahama Islands.**
Joseph H. Riley. In: *The Bahama Islands*. George Burbank Shattuck. New York: Macmillan, 1905, p. 347-68.
In this chapter, Riley begins by outlining ornithological expeditions to the Bahamas between 1731 and 1903. The bulk of the chapter is given over to a list of the 204 species found. For each species, Riley provides both the Latin and common names and locations. There are brief descriptions for forty-four endemic species. Many of the species listed are found in the Turks and Caicos Islands and particular locations are noted in the main list.

134 **List of the birds collected by C.L. Winch in the Caicos Islands and Inagua, Bahamas, during January and February, and in Abaco, in March, 1891.**
Charles Barney Cory. *The Auk*, vol. 8, no. 4 (July 1891), p. 296-98.
Cory lists twenty-nine species from the Caicos Islands, twenty-one species from Inagua and thirty species from Abaco. There is, however, no commentary.

135 **The origin of the avifauna of the Bahamas.**
Frank Michler Chapman. *American Naturalist*, vol. 25, no. 294 (June 1891), p. 528-39.
Chapman discusses the 156 species and subspecies of birds recorded, up to the time of writing, in the Bahamian archipelago including the Turks and Caicos Islands. He deals in more detail with the twenty-four native species, and offers a number of theories to explain their existence.

136 A list of birds of the West Indies, including the Bahama Islands and the Greater and Lesser Antilles, excepting the islands of Tobago and Trinidad.
Charles Barney Cory.   Boston, Massachusetts: Estes & Lauriat, 1886. rev. ed. 34p.

As the title indicates, this is purely a list, with no descriptions or illustrations, of fifty-seven families of birds found throughout the Caribbean. Under each family, Cory has listed genus and species and has given locations for each.

Crustaceans

137 *Lasionectes entrichoma*, new genus, new species, (Crustacea: Remipedia) from anchialine caves in the Turks and Caicos, British West Indies.
Jill Yager, Frederick R. Schram.   *Proceedings of the Biological Society of Washington*, vol. 99, no. 1 (1986), p. 65-70.

The authors provide a detailed description, with drawings, of *Lasionectes entrichoma*, a new genus and species of remipedia, a small marine cave crustacean, discovered in the Turks and Caicos Islands.

138 **Remipedia. Part I. Systematics.**
Frederick R. Schram, Jill Yager, Michael J. Emerson.   San Diego, California: Society of Natural History, 1986. 60p. 2 maps. bibliog.
(Memoirs of the San Diego Society of Natural History, 15).

The authors provide a detailed analysis of each species of the relatively new crustacean Order Nectiopoda, first collected in the early 1980s from caves in the Bahamas and the Turks and Caicos Islands. Three known nectiopodans, one new species and one fossil species are described and compared. At the time of writing, further parts were unavailable for examination.

139 **Zoogeographic implications of *Bahadzia*, a hadziid amphipod crustacean recently described from anchialine caves in the Bahamas and Turks and Caicos Islands.**
John R. Holsinger, Dennis W. Williams, Jill Yager, Thomas M. Iliffe.   *Stygologia*, vol. 2, no. 1/2 (1986), p. 77-83.

The genus *Bahadzia* is composed of two species, *Bahadzia williamsi* and *Bahadzia stocki*, which are separated geographically by a distance of 700 kilometres and geologically by four deep marine channels. Despite this, their habitats in the Bahamas and the Turks and Caicos Islands are very similar. The authors discuss both this genus and others in the family Hadziidae from the Caribbean–Gulf of Mexico region and speculate on the origin of the genus *Bahadzia*. They conclude that *Bahadzia* is an ancient relict that has lived in a specialized anchialine cave environment since Mesozoic times when it diverged from an early hadziid fauna that was probably widespread in the old Tethyan seaway, a marine connection extending westward from the present Mediterranean region to the northern Gulf of Mexico–Caribbean region.

140   A new genus and two new species of subterranean amphipod crustaceans
       (Haziidae) from the Bahamas and Turks and Caicos Islands.
       John R. Holsinger, Jill Yager.   *Bijdragen tot de Dierkunde*, vol. 55,
       no. 2 (1985), p. 283-94.
Holsinger and Yager describe a new genus, *Bahadzia* and two new species of
amphipod, or beach flea, crustaceans from anchialine caves in the Bahamas and the
Turks and Caicos Islands. The genus and species are described in detail with
accompanying drawings. The Turks and Caicos species, *Bahadzia stocki*, was found in
two caves on Providenciales.

141   A representative of the mainly abyssal family Pardaliscidae (Crustacea,
       Amphipoda) in cave waters of the Caicos Islands.
       Jan H. Stock, Jan J. Vermeulen.   *Bijdragen tot de Dierkunde*, vol. 52,
       no. 1 (1982), p. 3-12.
A new genus and species of Amphipoda is described from cave waters on
Providenciales as *Spelaeonicippe provo*. Detailed illustrations are provided. The
authors also discuss the possibility of an evolutionary link between this species and
another, belonging to the same new genus, found in a cave on Lanzarote in the Canary
Islands.

142   Cave shrimps in the Caicos Islands.
       Donald W. Buden, Darryl L. Felder.   *Proceedings of the Biological
       Society of Washington*, vol. 90, no. 1 (1977), p. 108-15.
Buden and Felder examine the cave shrimp species *Typhlatya garciai* Chace and
Barbouria cubensis (Von Martens) taken from the island of Providenciales and discuss
their distribution and habitat.

Reptiles

143   Notes on the natural history of the Caicos Islands dwarf boa,
       Tropidophis greenwayi.
       John B. Iverson.   *Caribbean Journal of Science*, vol. 22, no. 3/4
       (1986), p. 191-98.
The Caicos Islands dwarf boa was first described in 1936. It is the least known of the
species and is found on only six islands in the Caicos archipelago. Iverson discusses
distribution, habitat, size and growth, reproduction, food and feeding, defensive
behaviour, and the need for conservation and protection. His observations are based
on visits in 1976, 1978 and 1979.

144 **Feeding strategy of the Caicos ground iguana** *Cyclura carinata.*
Walter A. Auffenberg.   In: *Iguanas of the world: their behavior,*
ecology, and conservation. Edited by Gordon M. Burghardt, A. Stanley
Rand. Park Ridge, New Jersey: Noyes, 1982, p. 84-116. (Animal
Behavior, Ecology, Conservation, and Management).

Cyclura carinata, a small iguana restricted to the most southern of the Bahama Islands
and the Turks and Caicos Islands, is one of relatively few iguanas which eats plants.
This chapter reports the results of a study of the diet and feeding habits of this species
carried out intermittently on Pine Cay from July 1973 through to the end of August
1975. Auffenberg discusses ingestion, passage rates of food, foray patterns, caloric
values and annual yield of common food species.

145 **The thermal biology of the Turks and Caicos Islands rock iguana**
Cyclura carinata.
David Leslie Auth.   PhD thesis, University of Florida, Gainesville,
Florida, 1980. (Available from University Microfilms, Ann Arbor,
Michigan, order no. 80-29042).

This thesis is the result of Auth's investigations of *Cyclura carinata*, a large, tropical,
herbivorous iguana lizard. His studies of the lizard's ecological, ethological and
physiological thermal biology were carried out on Water Cay in the Caicos Islands and
at Gainesville, Florida between June 1974 and September 1976.

146 **Behavior and ecology of the rock iguana,** *Cyclura carinata.*
John B. Iverson.   *Bulletin of the Florida State Museum, Biological*
Sciences, vol. 24, no. 3, (Dec. 20, 1979), p. 175-358.

This is the author's 1977 PhD thesis from the University of Florida reprinted as an
issue of the *Bulletin of the Florida State Museum, Biological Sciences*. In it, he reports
on his study of the natural history and social ecology of the rock iguana carried out
between September 1973 and July 1976. Iverson's study had four major goals: to
obtain data on the behaviour, the adaptation, the life history and the community role
of a species; to determine what factors limit population size; to discover the methods
by which a species might survive co-habitation with man without the threat of
extinction; and to provide an in-depth charter study for extrapolation to similar
investigations of other species of *Cyclura* in the West Indies. His work includes
chapters on morphology, habitat, reproduction, growth, food and feeding, activity and
movement, social organization, interspecific co-actions (i.e. the relations that exist
between species in an ecological community), and density and demography.

147 **The impact of feral cats and dogs on populations of the West Indian rock**
iguana *Cyclura carinata.*
John B. Iverson.   *Biological Conservation*, vol. 14 (1978), p. 63-73.

In this paper, the author relates the systematic extermination of the rock iguana on
Pine Cay following the introduction of cats and dogs. His study was conducted between
September 1973 and July 1976. Iverson discusses the killing habits of the cats and dogs
and points out that by March 1978 no iguanas were to be found on the island.

148 **A check-list of West Indian amphibians and reptiles.**
Albert S. Schwartz, Richard Thomas. Pittsburgh, Pennsylvania:
Carnegie Museum of Natural History, 1975. 216p. 7 maps. (Carnegie
Museum of Natural History. Special Publications, no. 1).
Schwartz lists 506 species. For each entry, he provides the current and original names;
the author, date and bibliographical citation for the first mention of the species;
information on distribution; and general remarks.

149 **A new species of the genus *Aristelliger* (Sauria: Gekkonidae) from the
Caicos Islands.**
Albert S. Schwartz. Ronald I. Crombie. *Proceedings of the Biological
Society of Washington*, vol. 88, no. 27 (1975), p. 305-14.
Schwartz provides a very detailed description of a new species, *Aristelliger hechti*,
following some background information on previous reports of gecko lizards on the
Caicos Islands.

150 **A new subspecies of *Tropidophis greenwayi* from the Caicos Bank.**
Albert S. Schwartz. *Breviora*, vol. 194 (1963), p. 1-6.
This is a very detailed description of *Tropidophis greenwayi lanthanus*, a new
subspecies of small boa known only from South Caicos Island and the adjacent Long
Cay on the Caicos Bank. This is the first new boa find since 1936.

151 **Iguanas, snakes, and alligators, in the Turks Islands.**
Henry Brougham Guppy. In: *Plants, seeds, and currents in the West
Indies and Azores*. Henry Brougham Guppy. London: Williams &
Norgate, 1917, p. 486-87.
Guppy asserts that iguanas, snakes and alligators were once found throughout the
Turks Islands. In this brief article, he indicates that iguanas are now only found on
Long Cay and Greater Sand Cay, that snakes are confined to Eastern Cay and that
alligators have disappeared completely.

Insects

152 **Dragonflies of the Florida Peninsula, Bermuda, and the Bahamas.**
Sidney W. Dunkle. Gainesville, Florida: Scientific, 1989. 155p.
2 maps. bibliog.
Dunkle provides a very good introduction, outlining the anatomy and life history of the
dragonfly, along with information on photographing and collecting specimens. In the
main body of the work, he examines ninety-four dragonfly species. Each entry gives a
description and information on distribution, breeding habits, flight season, feeding,
mating and egg laying. There are 127 excellent colour photographs and three
checklists: one for the Florida Peninsula, one for Bermuda and one for the Bahamas,
including the Turks and Caicos Islands.

153 **Butterflies of T & C.**
Robert St. Leger. *Turks & Caicos Current*, vol. 2, no. 1 (Nov./Dec. 1983), p. 48-49, 51, 53, 55-56.
St. Leger describes thirty-seven species. Each entry includes the scientific name, a description and an indication of the distribution.

154 **A field guide to the butterflies of the West Indies.**
Norman D. Riley. London: Collins, 1975. 224p. map. bibliog.
Riley has produced a guide to allow for the identification of butterflies with a minimum of difficulty. He provides an introduction to butterfly morphology and classification, along with information on the life cycle of the butterfly and collecting methodologies. In the main body of the book, Riley gives descriptive information on 293 species. Each entry includes the scientific and common names, a description and an indication of distribution. A glossary, a checklist and a distribution table are also included. Of the species described, fifty-five are found in the Bahamas and the Turks and Caicos Islands.

155 **The butterflies of the Van Voast-American Museum of Natural History expedition to the Bahama Islands, British West Indies.**
Frederick H. Rindge. *American Museum Novitates*, no. 1715 (Mar. 25, 1955), p. 1-20.
This report is based on a collection expedition undertaken throughout the Bahamas and the Turks and Caicos Islands from December 1952 to May 1953. The members of the expedition collected 654 specimens and concluded that sixty-two species of butterfly were present in the region. This article includes descriptions of more than forty of these species.

156 **The butterflies of the Bahama Islands, British West Indies (Lepidoptera).**
Frederick H. Rindge. *American Museum Novitates*, no. 1563 (May 12, 1952), p. 1-18.
Rindge describes fifty-four species and subspecies of butterflies found throughout the Bahamian archipelago.

Prehistory and Archaeology

General

157 **Archaeological investigations within the Bahamas archipelago.**
John Winters, Julian Granberry, Art Leibold. In: *Proceedings of the Tenth International Congress for the Study of the Pre-Columbian Cultures of the Lesser Antilles.* Montreal: Centre de Recherches Caraibes, 1985, p. 83-92.

In this paper, the authors write about the cultural heritage of the Lucayan Indians. Initially, these Indians were seasonal visitors but ceramic evidence found in the archipelago has led these authors to conclude that slow, permanent migration began around 900 AD.

158 **Pre-historic Caicos.**
Shaun Dorsey Sullivan. *Turks & Caicos Current,* vol. 1, no. 7 (July/August 1982), p. 31, 33-34, 44.

Sullivan briefly outlines previous archaeological expeditions to the Caicos Islands. Based on his own work and the work of others, he concludes that Arawak Indians began to visit the islands around 750 AD and established permanent settlements about 950 AD.

159 **Prehistoric patterns of exploitation and colonization in the Turks and Caicos Islands.**
Shaun Dorsey Sullivan. PhD thesis, University of Illinois at Urbana-Champaign, Urbana, Illinois, 1981. (Available from University Microfilms, Ann Arbor, Michigan, order no. 82-03607.)

Sullivan reports on an archaeological and environmental survey of the Turks and Caicos Islands conducted between 1976 and 1980. His research is intended to expand the archaeological database concerning the prehistory of the islands. Forty-one prehistoric sites were located and surface collections made. Test excavations were conducted at nine sites and a detailed topographic map was made of one of them. Environmental resource surveys were also made of each island on which prehistoric sites were encountered. The data analysis indicates that there were two primary cultural periods. During the first, 750-950 AD, Arawak voyagers from the Greater Antilles made seasonal forays to the islands for salt. The second period, 950-1500 AD, saw the establishment of large permanent villages.

160   A brief history of Bahamian archeology.
       Julian Granberry.   *The Florida Anthropologist*, vol. 33, no. 3 (Sept. 1980), p. 83-93.
Granberry describes and discusses both archaological investigations of the Bahamas and the Turks and Caicos Islands and collections of artifacts gathered since the late 1880s.

161   An overview of the 1976 to 1978 archeological investigations in the Caicos Islands.
       Shaun Dorsey Sullivan.   *The Florida Anthropologist*, vol. 33, no. 3 (Sept. 1980), p. 120-42.
This article is based on ten months of archaeological surveys and test excavations conducted by Sullivan and forty-one volunteers between August 1976 and August 1978. Sullivan provides a broad outline of the results of the investigations, which were focused on Middle Caicos where thirty-five aboriginal sites were discovered; this article gives detailed descriptions of several of them. Sullivan and his team investigated ceramic finds and the place of salt in the diet and economy of the early Arawak Indians. He concludes that Arawak expansion in the Caribbean was the product of the exploitation of the resources of individual islands rather than simply the overflow from previously held territory.

162   **Bahamas prehistory.**
       William H. Sears, Shaun Dorsey Sullivan.   *American Antiquity*, vol. 43, no. 1 (Jan. 1978), p. 3-25.
The authors' investigations of prehistoric excavations in the Bahamas archipelago reveal that Antillean Lucayans migrated to the region between 800 and 1000 AD. They conclude that the Lucayans originally visited the area in search of concentrations of crystalline salt which were to be found in the Caicos Islands. Occupation of the area followed within a century based on an economy of mixed agriculture and the long distance trade in salt and dried conch. Sears and Sullivan also discuss the evolution of native ceramics.

163   **On the trail of the Arawaks.**
       Fred Olsen.   Norman, Oklahoma: University of Oklahoma Press, 1974. 408p. 16 maps. bibliog. (The Civilization of the American Indian Series, vol. 129).
This quite readable book is a personal account of the author's efforts to trace the origin of the people who inhabited the Antilles at the time of the first European contact. Although there is no specific mention of the Turks and Caicos Islands, Olsen's book is still useful as background information on the peoples of the Caribbean region.

164 **Sea diver, a quest for history under the sea.**
Marion Clayton Link.   New York: Rinehart, 1959. 333p. 5 maps.
bibliog.

This book describes the adventures and discoveries of the Link family skin diving expeditions, first in the Florida Keys and later the Bahamas. It incorporates useful information about underwater salvage methods and equipment and some colourful reconstructions of New World maritime history. Link gives accounts of searching for Columbus' *Santa Maria* off the north coast of Haiti, treasure hunting in the Silver Shoals to the southeast of the Turks Islands and tracking Columbus' route through the Turks and Caicos Islands.

165 **The cultural position of the Bahamas in Caribbean archaeology.**
Julian Granberry.   *American Antiquity*, vol. 22, no.2 (Oct. 1956),
p. 128-34.

Granberry briefly discusses archaeological surveys carried out in the Bahamas, including the Turks and Caicos Islands, between 1887 and 1955. He points out that of the sixty-one major prehistoric sites located throughout the archipelago, sixteen are open village sites, without stockade or fortifications. Of these sixteen, fifteen are found in the Caicos Islands group. He concludes that this concentration is a result of denser prehistoric population in the southern extremes of the archipelago and more thorough archaeological work in this area. Granberry also discusses the two distinct ceramic styles, Meillac and Carrier, both of which are found in the Turks and Caicos Islands. Finally, he shows the close prehistory relationship with Haiti which is most evident in the southern Bahamas/Turks and Caicos Islands.

166 **Origins of Tainan culture, West Indies.**
Sven Loven.   Gothenburg, Sweden: Elanders boktryckeri aktiebolag,
1935; New York: AMS, 1979. 696p. map.

Loven's work was originally published in 1924 under the title, *Über die wurzeln der tainischen kultur*. It is organized by topic, such as immigration in the West Indies, stone artifacts, ceramics, towns and houses, agriculture, fishing, social conditions, burial customs and religion. There is some information on the Turks and Caicos Islands though it is often combined with information on the Bahamas. Generally, the work is useful for background information.

167 **Central American and West Indian archaeology; being an introduction
to the archaeology of the states of Nicaragua, Costa Rica, Panama and
the West Indies.**
Thomas Athol Joyce.   London: P.L. Warner; New York: G.P.
Putnam's Sons, 1916; Freeport, New York: Books for Libraries, 1971.
270p. 2 maps. bibliog.

Joyce's book is divided into two sections: southern Central America and the West Indies. There is information on the Lucayans though nothing specific on the Turks and Caicos Islands. The book is useful for background information and as an introduction, to and summary of, excavations and discoveries prior to 1916.

168   **Lucayan remains on the Caicos Islands.**
Theodoor Hendrik Nikolaas de Booy. *American Anthropologist*,
vol. 14, no. 1 (Jan./Mar., 1912), p. 81-105.

In this general discussion of the Lucayans, de Booy pays particular attention to
excavations and finds on the Island of Providenciales, the Ambergris Cays, North
Caicos Island, Grand Caicos Island and East Caicos Island. De Booy describes
nineteen sites and the primary finds which consist of pottery and ceramic fragments,
stone idols and petroglyphs. He also comments on the origins and demise of these
early Caribbean natives.

169   **On the Lucayan Indians.**
William Keith Brooks. *National Academy of Sciences Memoirs*,
vol. 4 (1889), p. 215-22.

Brooks offers a short introduction to the Lucayan Indians and provides a detailed
examination of three Lucayan skulls, which are illustrated by twelve black-and-white
plates following p. 222.

170   **[Some stone implements from Honduras and Turks and Caicos Islands].**
Melfort Campbell. *The Journal of the Anthropological Institute of
Great Britain and Ireland*, vol. 6 (1876), p. 37-40.

This communication to the Anthropological Institute includes references to three celts,
one of jadeite and two of diorite, found on the Turks and Caicos Islands. Campbell has
also reprinted a letter, dated 10 August 1874, published by George Gibbs in the
newspaper, *Turks Island Standard*, concerning the antiquities of the Turks and Caicos
Islands.

The Molasses Reef wreck

171   **Analysis of the ballast of the Molasses Reef wreck.**
William Reginald Lamb, Donald Hart Keith, Susan A. Judy. *National
Geographic Research*, vol. 6, no. 3 (Summer 1990), p. 291-305.

Nearly 1,200 samples from the stone ballast were examined for evidence of the origin
and voyage history of this Spanish vessel, shipwrecked in the 1500s. The ballast was
systematically tested and cross-sections of the ballast mound were mapped *in situ*. The
investigators were able to identify five major and two undifferentiated rock groups.
Their analysis of the ballast mound yielded clues to the ship's size, the hull shape and
the ship's path prior to the wrecking event.

172   **The Molasses Reef wreck.**
Donald Hart Keith.   PhD thesis, Texas A & M University, College
Station, 1987. (Available from University Microfilms, Ann Arbor,
Michigan, order no. 88-08775.)
This two-volume thesis describes in detail the work done in excavating the wreck on
the Molasses Reef. Following a literature review, a history of the project and a survey
of the geographical setting, Keith provides detail concerning the ship itself, the ballast,
the anchors, the armaments and the ceramic and glass artifacts which have been found.

173   **The Molasses Reef wreck: a study of the essential elements of nautical
archaeology in the Caribbean.**
Donald Hart Keith.   In: *Underwater archaeology: proceedings of the
14th Conference on Underwater Archaeology*. Edited by Calvin R.
Cummings. San Marino, California: Fathom Eight, 1986, p. 94-97.
(Special Publication, no. 7.)
Keith gives a short but concise outline of the methods of exploration and excavation of
the Molasses Reef wreck.

174   **Analysis of hull remains, ballast and artifact distribution of a 16th-
century shipwreck, Molasses Reef, British West Indies.**
Donald Hart Keith, Joseph J. Simmons.   *Journal of Field
Archaeology*, vol. 12, no. 4 (Winter 1985), p. 411-24.
This paper is the culmination of three seasons of excavations. The authors describe the
field methods used for recording the distribution of components within the site area
and present their results. A number of helpful diagrams and charts accompany the
article.

175   **The Molasses Reef wreck, Turks and Caicos Islands, B.W.I.**
Donald Hart Keith, James A. Duff, Steven R. James, Thomas J.
Oertling, Joseph J. Simmons.   *International Journal of Nautical
Archaeology and Underwater Exploration*, vol. 13, no. 1 (1984), p. 45-
63.
The authors outline the work that has been done in the first two years of excavation,
describing the site history and the various artifacts, artillery pieces and shot, lead
objects, and hull remains that have been salvaged from the wreck.

176   **Scientists comb shipwreck – is it Columbus' Pinta?**
Mike Toner.   *Miami Herald*, (June 1, 1983), Section E, p. 1.
Toner describes what is known about this shipwreck and the means to date it,
suggesting that evidence indicates that the ship sank between 1500 and 1550. Toner
deduces that it was heavily armed with fifteen cannon and, although nothing points to
it as being the *Pinta*, there is nothing to say it is not the oldest documented shipwreck
in the Americas. At this point, radiochemical dating was being explored and coral
growth was also seen as a means of dating the wreck.

Prehistory and Archaeology. The Molasses Reef wreck

177 **Discord and discovery: has the *Pinta* been found?**
Connie Crowther. *Americas*, vol. 34, no. 5 (Sept./Oct. 1982), p. 3-8.
This is a good introduction to the Molasses Reef wreck originally found in 1977 by Olin Frick and John Gasque. Based on their own investigations, Frick and Gasque were convinced that the Molasses Reef wreck was Christopher Columbus' *Pinta* although Crowther points out that this has been disputed by Donald Keith and Sumner Gerard of the Institute of Nautical Archaeology.

178 **The *Pinta*?**
Pete Earley. *The Washington Post*, (Aug. 15, 1982), section H, p. 1, 4-5.
This extensive newspaper article details the work done by Olin Frick and John Gasque in investigating the identity of the shipwreck found off Molasses Reef and outlines their attempts to raise funds to salvage the ship. Earley also presents information concerning the difficulties between the Institute of Nautical Archaeology and Frick and Gasque in this salvage operation.

179 **Armed divers may have looted shipwreck claimed to be *Pinta*.**
Pete Earley. *The Washington Post*, (Nov. 27, 1981), section A, p. 4.
This is a newspaper report on the problems between the Institute of Nautical Archaeology and Olin Frick and John Gasque concerning the recovery of the wrecked ship which Frick and Gasque claimed to be Columbus' *Pinta*.

180 **Is shipwreck Columbus' Pinta?**
Mike Toner. *Miami Herald*, (Oct. 12, 1980), Section A, p. 1, 34.
Toner describes the initial efforts of Olin Frick and John Gasque in recovering the Molasses Reef wreck which they believed to be Columbus' *Pinta*.

History

Caribbean/West Indies

181 The modern Caribbean.
Edited by Franklin W. Knight, Colin A. Palmer.   Chapel Hill, North
Carolina: University of North Carolina Press, 1989. 382p. map. bibliog.
This work, comprising thirteen essays by Caribbean studies specialists, provides
background for the history and culture of the region. There are essays dealing with
labour, politics, the economy, literature, international relations, race and Caribbean
migration.

**182 Main currents in Caribbean thought: the historical evolution of
Caribbean society in its ideological aspects, 1492-1900.**
Gordon K. Lewis.   Baltimore, Maryland: Johns Hopkins University
Press, 1983. 375p.
Lewis explores the sixteenth and seventeenth century beginnings of Caribbean
thought, pro- and anti-slavery ideologies, the growth of nationalist and anti-colonialist
sentiment in the nineteenth century, and the development of secret religious cults. He
is able to show how European, African and Asian ideas have become Creolized and
Americanized thereby creating a new ideology. Although there is no bibliography,
Lewis does provide a large section of notes.

183 A short history of the West Indies.
John Horace Parry, Philip Manderson Sherlock.   London: Macmillan,
1971. 3rd ed. 337p. bibliog.
First published in 1956, this work is a valuable introduction to West Indian history.
Parry and Sherlock begin with the arrival of Columbus and trace West Indian history
through to independence in most of the British Caribbean. In their introduction, the
authors state that the 'history is worth studying for its own sake and not merely as an
appendix to the history of . . . European, African or Asian homelands, or of the

45

United States. Such a study, of the history of the West Indies in its own right, is the object of this book'. This objective has been admirably achieved.

184 **From Columbus to Castro: the history of the Caribbean, 1492-1966.**
Eric Eustace Williams.   New York: Harper & Row, 1970. 576p.
3 maps. bibliog.

Williams, Prime Minister of Trinidad and Tobago from 1956 to 1981, has written the first complete history of the Caribbean as a whole. He set out to collate all existing knowledge of the area in relation to the rest of the world and to provide, through a greater awareness of its heritage, a foundation for the economic integration of the region. Information on the Turks and Caicos Islands is limited but there is some mention of the Anglo-French struggle over control of the salt ponds in the eighteenth century.

185 **The growth of the modern West Indies.**
Gordon K. Lewis.   New York: Monthly Review Press, 1968. 506p.
map. bibliog.

Lewis provides a descriptive and interpretive analysis of the English-speaking Caribbean from 1918 to 1966. This work, organized along territorial and thematic lines, analyses in detail the various elements that make up the whole of West Indian society. Lewis makes brief mention of the Turks and Caicos Islands in conjunction with the islands' constitutional status, economy, isolation and neglect, and socio-economic patterns.

186 **West Indies.**
Philip Manderson Sherlock.   London: Thames & Hudson; New York: Walker, 1966. 215p. 3 maps. bibliog. (New Nations and People).

Sherlock divides his well-written, informative history of the British West Indies into two sections. The first half of the book gives a history of the region while the second half is a survey of social institutions such as the economy, the family, the Church, education, folklore and the arts. Sherlock emphasizes three decisive dates: 1650, when the production of sugar started to dominate Barbados; 1834, when slave emancipation was enforced throughout the West Indies; and the period 1938 to 1944, which led to home rule, federation and subsequently independence for most West Indian nations in the latter half of the twentieth century.

187 **History of the British West Indies.**
Alan Cuthbert Burns.   London: Allen & Unwin; New York: Barnes & Noble, 1965. 2nd ed. 849p. 30 maps. bibliog.

Burns' book is designed to give the general reader an outline history of the West Indies, from discovery to 1964, with particular emphasis on the British West Indies. The work is based on source material and is well documented. References to the Turks and Caicos Islands, more than in most general history books, are numerous. In particular, there are a number of references to the islands' constitutional state as it changed over the centuries. In addition, one of the appendixes lists the hurricanes that have swept through the region from 1495 to 1963 identifying those hurricanes which have struck the Turks and Caicos Islands.

188 **The history, civil and commercial, of the British West Indies. With a continuation to the present time.**
Bryan Edwards. London: T. Miller for G. and W.B. Whittaker, 1819; New York: AMS, 1966. 5th ed. 5 vols.

This work by Edwards is fascinating. A general description of the Bahama Islands, including the Turks and Caicos Islands, appears in volume four. Edwards provides information on early history, the Loyalists, geology, government, crops and industry, including the salt industry.

General

189 **The story of the Turks and Caicos Islands.**
C.D. Hutchings. Grand Turk: The Author, 1977. 7p.

This slim booklet provides a brief history of the islands. Hutchings concentrates on early Bermudian settlers and the salt trade, and the constitutional changes from 1848 to 1976. He also comments on the strategic location of the islands and the political importance this implies. In addition, mention is made of the conch trade and agriculture.

190 **Turks Islands landfall.**
H.E. Sadler. Grand Turk: The Author, 1975. 7 vols.

In seven volumes, Sadler discusses the history of the Turks and Caicos Islands from 1492 to the mid-1970s: Volume one, *Discovery, 1492-1605*; Volume two, *Shipwrecks, 1641-1953, Hurricanes, 1813-1960*; Volume three, *Piracy, 1605-1861*; Volume four, *Bermudian period, 1678-1776, King's agent, 1763-1840s*; Volume five, *Victorian age, 1845-1900*; Volume six, *Twentieth century, 1901-1952*; Volume seven, *Post-war period, 1945-1970s*. There is also an abridged, one-volume edition which not only deals with Columbus' first landfall in the Turks Islands but also with the Lucayans, early explorers and visitors to the islands, shipwrecks and the wrecking industry, and various hurricanes from 1795 to 1960. Sadler's work is not, however, scholarly; there is no bibliography, index, or footnotes. The photographs are poorly reproduced and rarely captioned. Despite this, the work is one of the few attempts at a history of the islands by an Islander. It is available from The Fortress, P.O. Box 31, Grand Turk, Turks and Caicos Islands, British West Indies.

191 **A report on the chief monuments of the Turks and Caicos Islands.**
David Buissert, Barrie Clark. *Bermuda Historical Quarterly*, vol. 31, no. 4 (Winter 1974), p. 90-92.

The authors briefly discuss the ruins of various forts and homes on the islands as well as government buildings and homes which are still being used. They call for a survey of all buildings of architectural and historical importance and recommend that these buildings be placed under some form of protection.

192 **A history of the Turks and Caicos Islands.**
Hosay Smith. Hamilton, Bermuda: [n.p.], 1968. 77p. map.

This unorganized, rambling history provides a great deal of information from the late nineteenth century and does include some fascinating points. However, the work could never be considered to be at all scholarly or professional. It is written as if Smith began to talk and his words were taken down verbatim whether or not successive sentences had anything to do with those that preceded them. Yet because of the lack of information in this area and because of some of the nineteenth-century statistics and lists of officials, this work does deserve to be examined by Turks and Caicos researchers.

Columbus' first landfall

193 **In quest of where America began: the case for Grand Turk.**
Josiah Marvel, Robert H. Power. *American History Illustrated*, vol. 25, no. 6 (Jan./Feb. 1991), p. 48-69.

Basing their conclusions on a variety of contemporary texts, Marvel and Power discuss in great detail their reasons for maintaining that Grand Turk was Columbus' first landfall.

194 **The Turks and Caicos Islands as possible landfall sites for Columbus.**
Robert H. Fuson. In: *Columbus and his world: proceedings of the first San Salvador Conference.* Compiled by Donald T. Gerace. Fort Lauderdale, Florida: College Center of the Finger Lakes, Bahamian Field Station, 1987. p. 173-84.

Fuson examines the six proposals which name various sites in the Turks and Caicos Islands as the landfall of Columbus. Despite the fact that in two separate articles published in 1961 he proposed South Caicos Island as the site of Columbus' landfall and then in 1982 proposed Grand Turk, Fuson changes his mind here and concludes that Samana Cay in the Bahamas was, in fact, the first landfall.

195 **Columbus landed on Caicos.**
Pieter H.G. Verhoog. In: *In the wake of Columbus: islands and controversy.* Edited by Louis De Vorsey, Jr., John Parker. Detroit, Michigan: Wayne State University Press, 1985. p. 29-34.

Using sailing directions from works by a variety of Columbus experts, Verhoog concludes that Columbus first landed on South Caicos Island. In this article, Verhoog briefly discusses his conclusions which were originally set forth in his *Guanahani again* (q.v.) and comments on his professional/academic rivalry with Samuel Eliot Morison, the Columbus biographer who concluded in his *Admiral of the ocean sea* (Boston, Massachusetts: Little, Brown, 1942) that Columbus landed on Watlings' Island in the Bahamas. Verhoog presents three of his original ten points to substantiate his claims.

196   **The Columbus landfall problem: a historical perspective.**
John Parker.   In: *In the wake of Columbus: islands and controversy*.
Edited by Louis De Vorsey, Jr., John Parker. Detroit, Michigan:
Wayne State University Press, 1985. p. 1-28.

In one of the most useful and concise examinations of the subject, Parker studies, in detail, all the major landfall theories from 1731 to 1981. Proponents of the various theories place the landfall on Cat Island, Watlings Island, Mayaguana, Samana Cay, the Plana Cays and Eleuthera, all in the Bahama Islands chain, as well as on Grand Turk Island and one of the Caicos Islands. Parker's article includes maps outlining twelve of the theories he examines.

197   **The discovery of Columbus's island passage to Cuba, October 12-27, 1492.**
Robert H. Power.   In: *In the wake of Columbus: islands and controversy*. Edited by Louis De Vorsey, Jr. John Parker. Detroit, Michigan: Wayne State University Press, 1985. p. 151-72.

In this article, Power attempts to identify Columbus' first landfall and to establish an original solution for Columbus' subsequent route to Cuba. He concludes that Grand Turk Island is the site of the first landfall by: looking at Columbus' route given the winds and currents at the time; examining environmental, geographical and other specific evidence from Columbus' *Journal* along with related documents describing Guanahani; and surveying the respective positions of Grand Turk and San Salvador Islands and their relationship to Cuba *vis-à-vis* the sailing directions outlined in the *Journal*. Power also discusses the work of those who advocate Grand Turk Island as well as various of the Caicos Islands.

198   **Grand Turk was Guanahani . . . and is San Salvador.**
Robert H. Fuson.   *Turks & Caicos Current*, vol. 1, no. 7 (July/Aug. 1982), p. 21, 23, 25, 27, 29-30.

In maintaining that Columbus first landed on Grand Turk Island, Fuson points out that Columbus named four major islands/island groups and one minor island chain before reaching Cuba. He also visited and measured but did not name one other large island. Fuson is convinced that earlier authors ignored this last fact when plotting Columbus' route through the Caribbean. Because of this, Fuson insists that others are incorrect, and when properly plotted, Columbus' route must begin with a first landfall on Grand Turk.

199   **Columbus never came.**
Kjeld Helweg-Larsen.   London: Jarrolds, 1963. 240p. 2 maps.

Helweg-Larsen contends that Columbus did not first land in the Bahamas but rather on one of the Caicos Islands. He bases his theory primarily on Verhoog's 1954 article (q.v.) which he quotes quite extensively. Helweg-Larsen also devotes three chapters to the Turks and Caicos Islands in which he provides a general description, an outline of early history and a discussion of the islands' future. He concludes that the islands would be better off with a more permanent link with the Bahamas.

200 **Caicos, confusion, conclusion.**
Robert H. Fuson. *Professional Geographer*, vol. 13, no. 5 (Sept. 1961), p. 35-37.

Fuson examines the six errors Doran (q.v.) accuses him of making and points out Doran's own mistakes. He also examines four of the islands described by Columbus and shows how they help support the theory that South Caicos Island is Columbus' San Salvador.

201 **Caicos: site of Columbus' landfall.**
Robert H. Fuson. *Professional Geographer*, vol. 13, no. 2 (March 1961), p. 6-9.

Using fifteenth-century sources, Fuson concludes, quite emphatically, that Columbus first landed in the New World on South Caicos Island and then travelled on to the Bahamas, Cuba and Hispaniola. He agrees completely with the information presented in Verhoog's 1954 article (q.v.). Fuson finds Verhoog's proofs 'intriguing' and sees his own article as 'a defense of Verhoog's hypothesis' (p. 7).

202 **This Columbus–Caicos confusion.**
Edwin Doran. *Professional Geographer*, vol. 13, no. 4 (July 1961), p. 32-34.

Doran refutes Fuson's March 1961 article (q.v.). He finds and discusses six errors in Fuson's argument and shows why Watlings Island in the Bahamas is the first landfall.

203 **A new theory on Columbus's voyage through the Bahamas.**
Edwin Albert Link, Marion Clayton Link. Washington, DC: Smithsonian Institution, 1958. 45p. map. bibliog. (Smithsonian Institution. Smithsonian Miscellaneous Collections, vol. 135, no. 4).

Following up on the work of Verhoog's 1947 book (q.v.) and 1954 article (q.v.), the authors searched past and present charts, studied original source material, reflected on the studies and opinions of other historians and made a personal reconnaissance by air and by sea. In light of their research, they mapped a new course for Columbus through the Bahamas and concluded that he landed on one of the Caicos Islands rather than on Watlings Island in the Bahamas. On their expedition, the Links paid less attention to distances than to the elapse of sailing time according to Columbus' *Journal*.

204 **Columbus landed on Caicos.**
Pieter H.G. Verhoog. *Proceedings of the United States Naval Institute*, vol. 80, no. 10 (Oct. 1954), p. 1101-11.

Using what he considers to be sailing directions found in Columbus' *Journal* and Columbus' descriptions of the four islands he visited before reaching Cuba and Espanola, Verhoog concludes that South Caicos Island was Columbus' first landfall in the New World. He also provides a list of ten points to confirm his conclusion.

205 **Guanahani again: the landfall of Columbus in 1492.**
Pieter H.G. Verhoog.   Amsterdam: C. De Boer, 1947. 66p. 2 maps.
Verhoog rejected the use of old maps and notations in trying to determine Columbus'
landfall and relied only on sailing directions, which he then plotted on a map in order
to trace Columbus' voyage. Using this plotting chart, an entirely new methodology, he
concluded that South Caicos Island was the first landfall. The book includes extensive
notes but no bibliography.

206 **On the possibility of determining the first landfall of Columbus by**
archaeological research.
Theodoor Hendrik Nikolaas de Booy.   *Hispanic American*
Historical Review, vol. 2, no. 1 (Feb. 1919), p. 55-61.
De Booy begins his research with the translation of Columbus' *Journal* which appears
in Gustavus Vasa Fox's 1882 booklet, *An attempt to solve the problem of the first*
landing place of Columbus in the New World (Washington, DC: Government Printing
Office). Fox had come to the conclusion that Samana or Atwood Cay in the Bahamas
was the site of the first landfall. Based on one sentence from the *Journal*, de Booy is
convinced that archaeological research will solve the landfall problem but comes to no
conclusion himself. He suggests that Columbus may well have landed on South Caicos
or Grand Turk but also suggests that Rum Cay, Samana Cay, East Plana Cay or West
Plana Cay, all in the Bahamas, might also lay claim as the site of the first landfall.

207 **Select letters of Christopher Columbus, with other original documents,**
relating to his first four voyages to the New World.
Christopher Columbus, translated and edited by Richard Henry
Major.   London: Hakluyt Society, 1847. 240p.
In this first edition of *Select letters* . . ., Major suggests that Columbus made his first
landfall on Grand Turk Island. He was heavily influenced by Gibbs' 1846 *Observations*
. . . (q.v.) and it was not until the publication of Alexander Becher's *The landfall of*
Columbus on his first voyage to America (London: J.D. Potter, 1856) that Major
rethought his position and concluded that Columbus first landed on Watlings Island in
the Bahamas. In the second edition of *Select letters* . . . (London: Hakluyt Society,
1870) Major announced his change of opinion. This first edition contains five letters by
Columbus describing the first, third and fourth voyages; a letter by Dr. Chanca,
physician to the fleet, describing the second voyage; and an extract from the will of
Diego Mendez, one of Columbus' officers during the fourth voyage, which gives a
detailed account of a number of adventures undertaken by himself but left undescribed
by Columbus.

208 **Observations tending to show that the Grand Turk Island, and not San**
Salvador, was the first spot on which Columbus landed in the New
World.
George Gibbs.   *Proceedings of the New York Historical Society*,
(1846), p. 137-48.
In order to come to the conclusion of the title, Gibbs used Columbus' *Journal* and
visited various Bahamian islands and the Turks and Caicos Islands. The San Salvador
in the title refers to Cat Island in the Bahamas. He also discusses other claims for the

first landfall throughout the article. Gibbs was a resident of Grand Turk Island which may have had some bearing on his insistence in the matter.

209 **Personal narrative of the first voyage of Christopher Columbus to America. From a manuscript recently discovered in Spain.**
Christopher Columbus.   Translated by Samuel Kettell. Boston, Massachusetts: Thomas B. Wait, 1827. 303p.

Kettell has translated a portion of Don Martin Fernandez de Navarette's *Coleccion de los Viages y Descubrimientos que hicieron por mar los Espanoles desde fines del Siglo XV* ('A collection of ocean voyages and discoveries made by the Spanish from the end of the 15th century'), originally published in Madrid in 1825. In a note on page 34, Kettell indicates quite clearly that he believes that Columbus' first landfall, Guanahani, was Grand Turk Island. Kettell bases his conclusion on Columbus' description of Guanahani and the sailing directions given in Navarette's narrative. This appears to be the first indication that one of the Turks and Caicos Islands may have been Columbus' first landfall.

1500 to the present

210 **Pirates and buccaneers of the Atlantic coast.**
Edward Rowe Snow.   Boston, Massachusetts: Yankee, 1944. 350p. map. bibliog.

This book is useful for its information on Edward Teach, 'Blackbeard' (d. 1718), and on Mary Read (d. 1720) and Anne Bonney (1700-20), the 'lady pirates'. Both Read and Bonney operated throughout the waters of the Bahamas and the Turks and Caicos Islands.

211 **Mary Read: the pirate wench.**
Frank Shay.   London: Hurst & Blackett, 1934. 286p.

This is a fictional account of the female pirate, Mary Read (d. 1720). Shay's book is an excellent narrative, historically accurate and straightforward.

212 **Mistress of the seas.**
John Carlova.   New York: Citadel, 1964. 253p.

This biography of Anne Bonney (1700-20), one of the 'lady pirates' is based on government documents, archival material, court records and newspaper accounts.

213 **Gunboat diplomacy of the government of George Grenville, 1764-1765: the Honduras, Turks Island and Gambian incidents.**
Nicholas Tracy.   *Historical Journal*, vol. 17, no. 4 (Dec. 1974), p. 711-31.

Although this article has more to do with George Grenville (1712-70) than the Turks and Caicos Islands, Tracy does shed some light on one incident in the islands' history. On 1 June 1764, a French man-of-war and several other vessels landed on Grand Turk Island, burnt and destroyed all the houses, carried off every person found, and seized fourteen small sailing vessels. Grenville, who was British Prime Minister from 1763 to

1765, readied war ships to meet the French invaders but the French soon abandoned the islands.

214 **A history of the Georgia Loyalists and the plantation period in the Turks and Caicos Islands.**
Charlene Johnson Kozy. DA thesis, Middle Tennessee State University, Murfreesboro, Tennessee, 1983. (Available from University Microfilms, Ann Arbor, Michigan, order no. 83-24428.)
Kozy's thesis traces the attitudes and behaviour of Georgia Loyalists during the American Revolution and their experience in exile, particularly in the Turks and Caicos Islands. The British government made ninety-six land grants in the Turks and Caicos Islands between 1789 and 1791 as compensation to those Loyalists who forfeited property as a result of fleeing the United States. Kozy offers an excellent view of the plantation life established in the islands and provides biographical information on twenty-five of the families who established these plantations. The plantation period in the Turks and Caicos Islands only lasted from 1789 to 1820. The failure of the plantations to thrive and survive was due to a combination of poor weather, insect infestation and, most of all, soil exhaustion.

215 **Tories transplanted: the Caribbean exile and plantation settlement of Southern Loyalists.**
Charlene Johnson Kozy. *The Georgia Historical Quarterly*, vol. 75, no. 1 (Spring 1991), p. 18-42.
Kozy outlines the efforts of the British government to find satisfactory tracts of land, primarily on Middle and North Caicos, for Georgian Loyalists and high-ranking military personnel. This is a wonderfully detailed account of who was given what land, and where and how much.

216 **My years in the sun: island memoirs.**
Denis Hermann Murphy. Lindenhurst, New York: The Author, 1983. 153p. map.
This account was written by Murphy in order to acquaint his children and grandchildren with the way of life in the Turks Islands in the early years of the twentieth century. Murphy was born into a family engaged in the salt trade on Grand Turk in 1902. The book begins with his birth and ends in 1929 when he left the islands for the United States. There are wonderful descriptions of the salt industry, island life, religious life and sports. There are also a number of early black-and-white photographs included. This item may be difficult to obtain. The author's address is 611 Grand Avenue, Lindenhurst, New York, 11757.

217 **Colonialism: the golden years.**
J.A. Golding. Ashford, England: Birlings, 1987. 258p. 3 maps.
Golding, born in Calcutta and raised in England, spent most of his professional life as a soldier and civil servant in Africa. However, he did spend some time in the mid-1960s as Administrator in the Turks and Caicos Islands. In the three chapters devoted to this particular assignment, Golding gives good descriptions of life in the islands and discusses, in some detail, development problems and the need for growth in the

tourism industry. There is also an amusing and colourful chapter on Queen Elizabeth II's 1966 visit to the islands.

218 **Paradise, Caicos-style: the development of Pine Cay.**
Don Keyote. *Turks & Caicos Current*, vol. 2, no. 5 (Jan./Feb. 1985), p. 13, 15, 17, 19, 21, 23, 25-28; vol. 2, no. 6 (March/April 1985), p. 27-36.
Keyote's two-part article provides a comprehensive history of the ups and downs of the development of the Pine Cay resort first proposed by Count Ferdinand Czermin in 1958.

Turks and Caicos Islands and Bermuda

219 **Turks & Caicos: an adventure backwards in time.**
Terry Tucker. *The Bermudian*, vol. 51, no. 10 (Nov. 1980), p. 19-23, 32, 35-39.
Tucker, a Bermudian writer and historian, wrote this article following a trip originally taken in 1975. She visited Grand Turk Island and Salt Cay to trace Bermuda's involvement in the salt industry which began in 1678. Tucker's article outlines the important historical and economic links with Bermuda.

220 **Bermuda today and yesterday, 1503-1973.**
Terry Tucker. Hamilton: Baxter's Ltd.; London: Robert Hale; New York: St. Martin's, 1975. 208p. 3 maps. bibliog.
This accessible, well-illustrated history of Bermuda includes several references to Bermudian involvement in the salt industry and trade based in the Turks and Caicos Islands.

221 **The Turks and Caicos Islands group in its relationship to Bermuda.**
Terry Tucker. *Bermuda Historical Quarterly*, vol. 31, no. 4 (Winter 1974), p. 78-89.
Following a brief sketch of the Turks and Caicos Islands, Tucker provides an excellent description of the early saltrakers from Bermuda and their activities in the islands. Particular emphasis is paid to Salt Cay and Grand Turk Island. Tucker also includes some interesting insights into the islands' early history from the mid-1600s to the mid-1800s.

222   **Bermuda from sail to steam: the history of the island from 1784 to 1901.**
      Henry Campbell Wilkinson.   London: Oxford University Press, 1973.
      2 vols. map. bibliog.
This detailed history of Bermuda does provide some information about the salt
industry and wrecking in the Turks and Caicos Islands, as well as some information
about problems between Bermuda and the Bahamas concerning jurisdiction over the
islands.

223   **The story of Bermuda and her people.**
      William Sears Zuill.   London: Macmillan, 1973. 240p. 13 maps.
      bibliog.
This easy-to-read history covers Bermuda from 1609 to 1970 and provides information
on the salt trade in the Turks and Caicos Islands and the difficulties between Bermuda
and the Bahamas over jurisdiction of the islands.

224   **Bermuda, salt, and the Turks Islands.**
      William Sears Zuill.   *Bermuda Historical Quarterly*, vol. 8, no. 4
      (Oct./Dec. 1951), p. 162-68.
Zuill outlines Bermuda's fight to retain control of the Turks Islands throughout the
eighteenth century. Unlike some other accounts of Bermudian interest in the salt
industry, Zuill discusses Bermuda's trade triangle. Salt was taken from the Turks
Islands to the British North American colonies and Newfoundland where it was sold
and grain and salt-fish purchased to be taken back to Bermuda. This trading sequence
became the backbone of Bermuda's economy.

225   **Bermuda in the old Empire: a history of the island from the dissolution
      of the Somers Island Company until the end of the American
      Revolutionary War, 1684-1784.**
      Henry Campbell Wilkinson.   London: Oxford University Press, 1950.
      457p. 2 maps. bibliog.
All of the references to the Turks and Caicos Islands in this history of Bermuda refer
to the salt trade. Wilkinson provides very good historical background material about
this industry.

226   **An historical and statistical account of the Bermudas, from their
      discovery to the present time.**
      William Frith Williams.   London: Thomas Cautley Newby, 1848.
      346p. map.
This history of Bermuda provides some information on the Turks and Caicos Islands.
In 1710, the Spanish took possession of Turks Island on which Bermudians had been
raking salt since 1678. Sometime between 1713 and 1715 (the records are not clear) a
Bermudian force under the command of Captain Lewis Middleton was dispatched to
regain possession. The expedition was successful.

227 **The question of the Bahama jurisdiction over the Turk's Islands discussed in a letter to the Honourable Speaker and gentlemen of His Majesty's Colonial Assembly of the Bermuda or Somer's Islands.**
John Harvey Tucker. *The Bermuda Historical Quarterly*, vol. 1, no. 1 (Jan./Feb./March 1944), p. 21-32; vol. 1, no. 2 (May/June/July 1944), p. 81-94; vol. 1, no. 3 (July/Aug./Sept. 1944), p. 127-37; vol. 1, no. 4 (Oct./Nov./Dec. 1944), p. 179-88; vol. 2, no. 1 (Jan./Feb./March 1945), p. 29-34.

These articles were first published as one document in London by F. Harding in 1803. Tucker, writing under the pseudonym of 'Isocrates', outlines, in fascinating detail, the reasons why Bermuda should retain its jurisdiction over the Turks and Caicos Islands. From vol. 1, no. 2 on, the article appears under the title, 'Bermuda's claim to Turk's [sic] Islands'.

Turks and Caicos Islands and the Bahamas

228 **The separation of the Turks and Caicos Islands from the Bahamas 1848.**
Patrice M. Williams. *Journal of the Bahamas Historical Society*, vol. 11, no. 1 (Oct. 1989), p. 12-15.

Williams, the Assistant Archivist of the Bahamas, discusses Bahamian jurisdiction over the Turks and Caicos Islands from the mid-eighteenth century to 1848 and describes the legislation pertaining to the islands at the time. In particular, she deals with the numerous petitions for secession presented by the Turks and Caicos Islanders to Great Britain between 1827 and 1847. The Islanders gave four reasons for wanting to secede: the islands were too far distant from Nassau to be properly governed; there was inadequate representation in the House of Assembly; there was unfair taxation; and changes in the salt pond leasing regulations were seen to be restrictive. In 1848 the Turks and Caicos Islands ceased to be governed by the Bahamas and became the responsibility of Jamaica.

229 **A history of the Bahamas.**
Michael Craton. Waterloo, Ontario: San Salvador Press, 1986. 3rd ed. 332p. 9 maps. bibliog.

Craton's book is the most authoritative history of the Bahamas and is essential for any Bahamian collection, large or small. Because the Turks and Caicos Islands were administered by the Bahamas from 1799 to 1848, Craton's history should also be included in any Turks and Caicos collection. There are a number of references to the islands including the Bahamian attempt to levy duties on Bermudian saltrakers in the early 1700s, the French invasions of the mid to late 1700s, and the Separation Act of 1848.

230   **The story of the Bahamas.**
      Paul Albury.   London: Macmillan Caribbean; New York: St. Martin's,
      1975. 294p. 6 maps. bibliog.
Albury, a Bahamian dentist and local historian, has written an overview of Bahamian
history from Columbus to 1973, the year of Bahamian independence. Like Craton's *A*
history of the Bahamas (q.v.), Albury's work includes several references to the Turks
and Caicos Islands. This non-scholarly work is enjoyable, easy to read and should be a
part of any Turks and Caicos collection.

231   **The early settlers of the Bahama Islands, with a brief account of the**
      American Revolution.
      Arnold Talbot Bethell.   Holt, England: Rounce & Wortley, 1930. 2nd
      ed. 166p.
In this history of the Bahamas, from the mid-seventeenth century to the early
twentieth century, Bethell provides a number of documents related to Bahamian
settlement. Many of these documents, as well as Bethell's own text, list the names of
the early settlers, making the work an excellent source of genealogical information.
Although Bethell does not devote any of his work directly to the Turks and Caicos
Islands, some of the lists of names include Loyalists who settled in the Turks and
Caicos Islands and the Loyalist background information is relevant. There is no index.

232   **The Bahamas.**
      R. Montgomery Martin.   In: *History of the West Indies: comprising*
      Jamaica, Honduras, Trinidad, Tobago, Grenada, the Bahamas, and the
      Virgin Islands. London: Whittaker, 1836, p. 274-87. (British Colonial
      Library, vol. 4).
Martin includes the Turks and Caicos Islands as an integral part of the Bahamian
archipelago in this short discussion of the history of the islands. He also includes
comments on geology, climate, population, produce and commerce, finance and
government.

Turks and Caicos Islands and Jamaica

233   **The story of Jamaica from prehistory to the present.**
      Clinton Vane de Brosse Black.   London: Collins, 1965. rev. ed. 255p.
      2 maps. bibliog.
Based on his *History of Jamaica*, published in 1958 (London: Collins, 256p.), Black has
concentrated on telling the island's story from prehistory to independence in 1962 in as
much detail as possible without interpreting that story for his readers. Although there
is little information about the Turks and Caicos Islands, this is a good, readable history
of Jamaica which will provide background information for the study of the relationship
between Jamaica and the Turks and Caicos Islands.

234 **A history of Jamaica from its discovery by Christopher Columbus to the year 1872.**
William James Gardner.   London: Stock, 1873; New York: Appleton, 1907; London: Cass, 1971. 510p. map. (Cass Library of West Indian Studies, no. 17).

Gardner's work is one of the most detailed of the histories of Jamaica written in the post-emancipation period. Gardner, a missionary/pastor in Jamaica from 1849 to 1874, divides Jamaican history into five major periods. Under each there are chapters devoted to historical events, commerce and agriculture, religion and education, and manners and customs. Like Black's *The story of Jamaica* . . . (q.v.), this work is useful for background information.

Drug Trade

235 **Bunglers' blues.**
P.J. O'Rourke. *Rolling Stone*, no. 452/453 (July 18-Aug. 1, 1985),
p. 41-42, 114-16.
This reporter makes a cursory attempt to probe the drug trade in the Turks and Caicos
Islands and to unearth background information on Norman Saunders, Chief Minister
of the islands who was arrested for drug trafficking in March 1985. This is an article
more of atmosphere than of fact.

236 **Cutting the Caicos connection.**
Peter Kiernan, Daniel Burke. *Macleans*, vol. 98, no. 11 (Mar. 18,
1985), p. 31.
Kiernan and Burke report on the arrest of the Turks and Caicos Islands' Chief Minister
and the Minister of Commerce and Development, a Turks and Caicos legislative
councillor and a Quebec businessman, all charged with conspiracy to import cocaine
and marijuana into the United States.

237 **Turks and Caicos: island in a stew.**
Economist, vol. 294, no. 7386 (Mar. 23, 1985), p. 42.
This short article reports on the arrest of Norman Saunders on charges of conspiring to
import narcotics into the United States. The unnamed author briefly comments on the
drug problem in the Turks and Caicos Islands and calls for Saunders' resignation.

238 **Bad day for *Benny*.**
Christopher Abel. *Proceedings of the United States Naval Institute*,
vol. 110, no. 9 (Sept. 1984), p. 30-34.
Abel documents the apprehension of the converted fishing vessel, *Benny*, by the Coast
Guard cutter, *Point Warde*, in June 1982 off the Turks Islands. The *Benny* was carrying
over ten tons of marijuana. Members of the crew, from both Cuba and Colombia,

were later convicted of smuggling and sent to jail for terms ranging from three to five years.

239 Sun, sand and contraband.
Patrick Skene Catling. *Telegraph Sunday Magazine*, no. 306 (Aug. 15, 1982), p. 16-19, 21, 25.

In this investigative article, Catling provides a fair amount of background information on the drug trade in the Turks and Caicos Islands, but still leaves a number of questions unanswered. There are interviews with a British Detective Inspector sent to assist the local police, and the Chief Minister, Norman Saunders. The latter interview, in which Saunders condemns drug trafficking, is most interesting given his subsequent arrest for drug trafficking in 1985.

240 The Caribbean connection.
Steve Dougherty, Robert Coram. *Caribbean and West Indies Chronicle*, vol. 96, no. 1556 (July 1980), p. 12-13, 27-28.

Dougherty and Coram investigate drug smuggling in the Turks and Caicos Islands in an article which consists of interviews with Governor John Strong, narcotics experts from Great Britain and some individuals involved in the smuggling itself.

Health

241 **Atlas of medicinal plants of Middle America, Bahamas to Yucatan.**
Julia F. Morton.   Springfield, Illinois: Charles C. Thomas, 1981.
1420p. bibliog.

Morton lists over 1000 medicinal plants grouped into more than 150 families in this study of a region which includes the Turks and Caicos Islands. The genera are listed alphabetically within each family and the species are listed alphabetically within each genus. For each species, she gives a detailed description and information on geographical origins and distribution; scientific and vernacular names; chemical constituents; the medicinal uses of the whole plant and its parts; the plant's properties and effects; and any other economic uses. The work is accompanied by over 500 high quality black-and-white photographs, a list of the plants classified according to principal uses, a scientific name index, a vernacular name index and an extensive bibliography.

242 **The nutritional status of children in the Turks and Caicos Islands.**
Mervyn D. Cohen, P. Morgan, P. Baker.   *West Indian Medical Journal*, vol. 23, no. 2 (June 1974), p. 92-97.

The authors undertook a survey in 1973 to assess the nutritional status of over 800 children in order to assist in formulating a government nutrition policy and to permit comparisons with other West Indian territories. All children were weighed and measured with a random one-third being chosen for haemoglobin estimation. Survey results showed that in the first year of life nutrition was excellent, and that children over five years of age were taller and heavier than most West Indians surveyed. The most important finding was the high prevalence of anaemia which suggested the need for iron supplements in the diet

243 **Microfilariasis in the Turks Islands.**
J.L. Stafford, K.R. Hill, E.L. de Montaigne.   *West Indian Medical Journal*, vol. 4, no. 3 (Sept. 1955), p. 183-87.

The purpose of this article is to record the incidental diagnosis of symptomless microfilariasis in two patients from the Turks Islands who were admitted to the Hansen Home Leprosarium in Jamaica for the treatment of chronic tuberculoid leprosy. Both patients were from the same island and were infected with the same species of microfilariasis, a larva which can cause elephantiasis. Cases such as this had not hitherto been reported in Jamaica or its dependencies and were the first reported incidences of filariasis in this region.

Government

244 **Turks and Caicos Islands commission of inquiry 1986: report of the Commissioner Mr. Louis Blom-Cooper QC into allegations of arson of a public building, corruption and related matters with appendices.**
Louis Blom-Cooper.   London: HMSO, 1986. 226p. 2 maps. bibliog. (Cm. 21.)

On New Year's Eve, 1985, a government-owned building on Grand Turk, Bascombe House, was burned to the ground. Arson was suspected, and investigations not only proved this to be true but also uncovered suspected government corruption. The Commission of Inquiry was established to examine all these allegations. This document includes a good introduction to the history and constitutional status of the Turks and Caicos Islands; an outline of the events of New Year's Eve, 1985; a discussion of corrupt and improper practices in the Public Works Department; a look at patronage in the islands; and Blom-Cooper's conclusions and recommendations.

245 **Government administration in a very small microstate: developing the Turks and Caicos Islands.**
John E. Kersell.   *Public Administration and Development*, vol. 8, no. 2 (April/June 1980), p. 169-81.

Kersell describes how the Turks and Caicos Islands have adapted the principles of the Westminster-Whitehall model to its particular conditions. The article contains discussions of history, geography, and economics as well as commentary on the government, the judiciary, politics, and future development. Kersell concludes that the islands have impressive development potential.

Foreign Relations

General

246 **Oh well, back to the bat droppings.**
Macleans, vol. 90, no. 12 (June 13, 1977), p. 60-61.
This is a whimsical, tongue-in-cheek article concerning squabbles between the Turks and Caicos Islands and the Dominican Republic over sunken treasure. The suggestion is made that Canada should adopt the Turks and Caicos Islands, and the islands should export manure from bat droppings in the caves on Grand Caicos Island.

Canada

247 **Canada and the Turks and Caicos Islands.**
Ian A. Stuart. *Canadian Parliamentary Review*, vol. 11, no. 2
(Summer 1988), p. 18-21.
Stuart outlines many of the steps that the proposed association with Canada has taken. Such an association with the Turks and Caicos Islands was first suggested in 1917 though serious attention was not paid until the mid-1970s. By 1986, a poll conducted on the islands indicated that ninety per cent of the inhabitants favoured some kind of association with Canada. However, a Canadian report (the Daubney Report) prepared in the same year concluded: that it was inappropriate for Canada unilaterally to institute formal talks with the Turks and Caicos Islands when an election was imminent on the islands; that Canada could not be seen to be interfering in the internal free democratic process of another country; that Canada could enter into talks with a newly elected Turks and Caicos government provided the new government asked for the talks and the British government gave its permission; that Canada should increase foreign trade to the Turks and Caicos Islands; and that the Canadian private sector should

consider investing in the islands. The article also outlines the forms such an association might take, the advantages of association for both countries, and the results of a survey conducted by one Canadian Member of Parliament on the proposed association.

248 **Paradise in the breezes.**
    Nora Underwood. *Macleans*, vol. 101, no. 12 (Mar. 14, 1988), p. 58.
Underwood provides some background to the proposed link between Canada and the Turks and Caicos Islands and outlines the advantages and disadvantages to such a link. She suggests that a connection between the two countries would help Canada's tourism deficit since the islands would use Canadian currency. However, Canada would have to assume the islands' $2,000,000 annual operating deficit which has traditionally been absorbed by Great Britain.

249 **Canada's fantasy islands.**
    Paul Gessell. *Macleans*, vol. 100, no. 13 (Mar. 30, 1987), p. 10-12.
Gessell discusses Canadian political movements in favour of an economic link between Canada and the Turks and Caicos Islands, as well as the doubts expressed by some Turks and Caicos politicians. He also outlines the efforts of the Turks and Caicos Development Organization, which promotes this economic connection, and its Toronto-based counterpart, the Canadian Turks and Caicos Islands Research and Development Corporation.

250 **Clouds over paradise.**
    Macleans, vol. 100, no. 18 (May 4, 1987), p. 14.
This unsigned article reports on a meeting held between representatives of the Turks and Caicos Development Organization and a Canadian government committee concerning the annexation of the islands by Canada. The article indicates that the Canadian government is non-committal because such an annexation could open Canada to charges of neo-colonialist activities. Annexation might also be seen as an expensive venture given the high rate of unemployment and the poor health services in the islands.

251 **A TCI connection.**
    John E. Kersell. *Policy Options*, vol. 8, no. 10 (Dec. 1987), p. 27-28.
Kersell begins his article by speculating that a government committed to achieving some sort of connection with Canada would no doubt be elected in 1988. He describes the Turks and Caicos Development Organization which sees the potential partners retaining independence but striking a mutually advantageous 'deal' whereby their societies, cultures and economies would complement each other. Kersell likens this arrangement to the associated states in the South Pacific, pointing out that Canada could offer educational and technical assistance, provide help to combat the Turks and Caicos drug problem, and give the islanders the means to a decent livelihood. In return, Canadians would be able to take advantage of the off-shore tax haven and tourism dollars would, in effect, stay within the Canadian economy.

252 **Don't disrupt this sunny tax haven.**
John Porteous. *Financial Post*, vol. 68 (June 1, 1974), p. 6.

Porteous presents the views of three groups of dissenters who wish to discourage union with Canada: the American businessmen who developed Providenciales, Canadians living in the islands who fear the loss of tax haven status and prosperous island fishermen and tradesmen. Porteous advises that the best form of involvement for Canadians is individual investment.

253 **Nova Scotia South? a Caribbean colony hopes to join Canada.**
John E. Cooney. *Wall Street Journal*, vol. 183, no. 45 (Mar. 6, 1974), p. 1, 37.

This newspaper article describes the efforts of Turks and Caicos Islanders to persuade Canada to take their country over as a territory or part of a province (Nova Scotia being the most likely candidate) or even as a national park.

254 **Our own gateway to Caribbean for the asking?**
John Partridge. *Financial Post*, vol. 68 (Feb. 2, 1974), p. 8.

Partridge presents the thoughts of C.W. (Liam) Maguire, a member of the Turks and Caicos State Council, on union with Canada. Maguire outlines the benefits to Canada (increased trade with and access to the Caribbean and South America) and to the Turks and Caicos Islands (increased economic development and access to Canadian judicial and educational systems).

255 **Place in the sun.**
Time (Canada), vol. 103 (Feb. 18, 1974), p. 7.

This short, unsigned article gives a brief report on a Turks and Caicos petition to the British government requesting association with Canada. Reactions in the United Kingdom and Canada are also included.

256 **Turks and Caicos Islands: Nova Scotia's new south shore?**
John Porteous. *Atlantic Advocate*, vol. 64, no. 10 (June 1974), p. 21-22.

Porteous opposes the plan for Canada to acquire the Turks and Caicos Islands. He outlines US involvement in the islands and indicates what the plan would mean to the Maritimes. Specifically, Porteous objects to the tax-free status of the islands as opposed to Canada's tax system, the high numbers of unemployed who would be added to Canada's welfare system, and the perception of Canada as an imperialist nation.

Constitution and Legal System

Constitution

257 **Turks and Caicos Islands: report of the Constitutional Commission.**
Great Britain. Constitutional Commissioner for the Turks and Caicos
Islands.   London: HMSO, 1987. 42p. (Cm. 111).
The three members of the Commission, Sir Roy Marshall, Henry Steele and Albert
Williams, were asked to formulate proposals for the constitutional future of the Turks
and Caicos Islands. This document contains background information and a history of
the islands, and the Commission's findings and recommendations. There are thirty-two
recommendations in total dealing with the Legislative Council, the ministerial system
of government, the Public Service, the Attorney General, the Ombudsman, prevention
of corruption, private practice by retired government officers, and planning and
development.

258 **The political and constitutional development of the Turks and Caicos
Islands (1946-1981).**
Conrad C. Higgs.   BA thesis, University of the West Indies, Kingston,
Jamaica, 1981.
Higgs provides a Turks Islander's view of constitutional development and political
advancement in the Turks and Caicos Islands during a period of great change in the
islands' history. He also offers suggestions for constitutional improvement and future
directions, and includes background information on early political parties in the
islands. This thesis is available at the University of the West Indies in Kingston and the
Victoria Public Library in Grand Turk.

259 **Turks and Caicos Islands: proposals for constitutional advance: report by the Constitutional Commissioner, the Rt. Hon. the Earl of Oxford and Asquith.**
Great Britain. Foreign and Commonwealth Office. London: HMSO, 1974. 31p.

This document contains an outline of the Earl of Oxford and Asquith's consultations during his six-week visit to the islands in 1973. Two-thirds of the item is devoted to the Earl's recommendations concerning the Governor, the Executive Council, the Legislative Assembly, the powers and procedures of the Legislative Assembly, and the Judiciary. The document also contains some historical background.

Legal system

260 **Turks and Caicos Islands consolidated index of statutes and subsidiary legislation to . . .**
Faculty of Law Library. University of the West Indies, Barbados. Bridgetown, Barbados: Faculty of Law Library, 1983-. annual.

This is one of a series in the West Indian Legislation Indexing Project (WILIP). The index lists statutes and subsidiary legislation in force since 8 April 1969.

261 **The Turks and Caicos Islands: a brief outline of the judicial organisation.**
Ena Woodstock. *Commonwealth Judicial Journal*, vol. 2, no. 2 (Dec. 1977), p. 11-13.

Woodstock provides a brief description of the political organization of the Turks and Caicos Islands, followed by a more extensive description of the judicial organization.

262 **The laws of the Turks and Caicos Islands containing the ordinances in force on the 8th day of April 1969 together with certain other enactments which are in force in the Islands.**
J.N. Glover. Grand Turk: Government of the Turks and Caicos Islands, 1970-72. rev. ed. 3 vols.

The first two volumes, published in 1970, contain the ordinances in force on 8 April 1969, while volume three, published in 1972, contains ordinances enacted between 8 April 1969 and 1 November 1971 along with an index. The three-volume edition also contains enactments of the Legislature of the Bahama Islands which still apply and some Jamaican laws which are still in force. This edition is supplemented by continuation volumes.

263   **An annotated edition of certain of the ordinances of the Turks and Caicos Islands from 1908-1940 with chronological tables.**
A.R. Dickson.   Kingston: Government Printer, 1944. 179p.

This work is divided into two parts. Part I consists of chronological tables of the ordinances and Part II provides references to 161 ordinances. Of this number, sixty-three are presented in full while the remainder are listed by title only. These 'title-only' ordinances include those that expired, were repealed or were disallowed between 1908 and 1940.

Economy and Finance

264 **Bahamas and the Turks and Caicos Islands.**
Great Britain. Department of Trade and Industry.   London:
Department of Trade and Industry, 1990. 43p. map. (Hints to
Exporters.)

This booklet, aimed at the foreign investor, is divided into three sections: the
Bahamas, the Turks and Caicos Islands and 'Additional information'. Unfortunately,
the Turks and Caicos Islands section is rather small and provides only brief information
on geography, economics, imports and exports, exchange control and documentation.
The addresses listed in section three are useful for further information.

265 **A nice niche at the crossroads.**
Norman Peagam.   *Euromoney*, supplement (May 1989), p. 101-16.

This section on the Turks and Caicos Islands is from a 116-page supplement which
outlines finance and investment in a number of Caribbean states. Peagam discusses the
possibility of the growth of such offshore financial institutions as holding companies,
insurance companies and banks. He points out the problems which will be encountered
as well as the potential to be found.

266 **Turks and Caicos.**
Gordon Cramb.   *Financial Times*, (Nov. 27, 1989), p. 29-33.

Almost twenty years after David Lascelles' *Financial Times* survey (q.v.), Cramb takes
another look at the Turks and Caicos Islands. In seven short articles, he examines the
general economic outlook, relations with the United Kingdom, banking and finance,
tourism, communication, industry and fisheries. There is also a glowing message from
Oswald Skippings who was elected the Chief Minister in March 1988.

267 **Turks and Caicos.**
Investment International, (July 1989), p. 51.
As the unnamed author points out, until recently, the Turks and Caicos Islands have been relatively under-used as a tax haven, though taxation is virtually non-existent. The new Companies Ordinance only came into existence in 1982 and efforts to develop the banking and finance sectors are fairly recent. Despite this, over 7,000 new companies had been set up in the islands since 1982.

268 **Caribbean economic handbook.**
Peter D. Fraser, Paul Hackett.   London: Euromonitor Publications, 1985. 241p. 10 maps.
The section on the Turks and Caicos Islands (p. 190-94) offers discussion of the economy, agriculture and industry, tourism and the finance industry. There are also statistical tables on population and government revenue and data tables comparing the islands with the rest of the Caribbean in the areas of population distribution, gross domestic product, tourist arrivals and exchange rates. Along with chapters on other individual countries, Fraser and Hackett also include general chapters on the Caribbean in world context along with an overview and future outlook for the region.

269 **An investor's guide to the Turks and Caicos Islands.**
Rupert S. Missick.   Grand Turk: The Turks and Caicos Pub. Co. Ltd., 1981. 50p. 3 maps.
This booklet provides information on the postal service, immigration and customs regulations, medical facilities, communication and transportation, the government and legal system and descriptions of the individual islands. Despite its age, the booklet is not terribly out-of-date. The publisher's address is P.O. Box 162, Grand Turk, Turks and Caicos Islands, British West Indies.

270 **Alexis Nihon wants island surf for casino turf.**
Anne Gregor.   *The Gazette* (Montreal), (Sept. 10, 1977), p. 29.
Canadian industrialist and businessman, Alexis Nihon, attempted to gain control of the island of Providenciales in order to develop a freeport and casino, but met with opposition to, and only lukewarm support for, this idea in the islands. Gregor describes Nihon's efforts.

271 **Turks and Caicos: *Financial Times* survey.**
David Lascelles.   *The Financial Times* (Oct. 22, 1970), p. 24-26.
In this survey, Lascelles presents four articles which give some financial background to present circumstances: 'The Caribbean's late developer', 'Islands seek tax haven status', 'Stable investment area – for the present' and 'Economic hopes pinned on tourism and property'.

272 **Economic survey and projection, Turks and Caicos.**
London: Ministry of Overseas Development, British Development Division in the Caribbean, 1969. 43p.
This document was prepared to provide an economic framework for discussion of the future aid requirements of the Turks and Caicos Islands and contains a great deal of economic information about the islands in the late 1960s. The survey focuses on

agriculture and fisheries, salt, transportation, hotels and tourism, construction and engineering and the economic impact of American military bases. There are thirty-two statistical tables which give figures for the early to late 1960s as well as projections up to the early 1970s.

273   **The Turks and Caicos Islands, B.W.I.**
        F.W. Fraser.   *Commercial Intelligence Journal*, vol. 44, no. 1419
        (April 11, 1931), p. 515-17.
Fraser gives information on the salt trade and steamship service between the islands and Canada. He also provides general import and export figures for 1925-29 and detailed figures for 1929.

Industry and Trade

General

274 **Kingston reports: Turks and Caicos Islands.**
W.D. Hutton. *Canadian Commerce*, vol. 136, no. 1 (Jan. 1972),
p. 21-22.
Hutton begins this brief article with a short history and description of the Turks and
Caicos Islands. The author's main purpose is to provide a discussion of industry: salt
raking, agriculture, fishing and tourism. The article also outlines the opportunities for
Canadian exporters which can be found in the islands.

275 **A Turks Island call for attention.**
H.A. Darrell. *Canada-West Indies Magazine*, vol. 20, no. 4 (March
1931), p. 108-09.
Darrell points out that island development has been neglected by Canadian industry
because it is not on the steamship routes between Canada and the rest of the West
Indies. There are also some comments on the salt and sponge industries.

Conch and fishing

276 **Fishing, an industry of potential and problems.**
Mohamed Hamaludin. *Turks & Caicos Current*, vol. 1, no. 9 (Nov./
Dec. 1982), p. 4-7.
The fishing industry is based primarily on South Caicos Island and involves three
distinct groups: the fishermen, the processing plant owners and the processing plant
workers. For the most part, Hamaludin discusses the problems of competition, over-
fishing and the lack of a government patrol boat. He points out that, if properly
supervised, the fishing industry, involving lobster and conch as well as scale fish, could
be extremely lucrative.

277 **The Caicos conch trade.**
Edwin Beal Doran. *Geographical Review*, vol. 48, no. 3 (July 1958),
p. 388-401.
In this highly readable article, Doran examines two very important aspects of the
conch trade. First, he looks at the conch trade and industry as an economic venture
and provides two tables of figures for dried conch exports in selected years between
1913 and 1956 and frozen conch exports for 1950 to 1956. Second, he comments on the
diffusion of cultural traits between the Caicos Islands and Haiti, one of the islands'
more important trading partners. Doran investigates how trade, no matter how small,
can encourage an exchange of cultural ideas. He concludes that this also happens
throughout the West Indies.

Insurance

278 **Turks and Caicos to enforce captive law: new rules could drive away
some insurers.**
Douglas McLeod. *Business Insurance*, vol. 24 (April 30, 1990),
p. 76-77.
The Turks and Caicos Insurance Ordinance of 1989 came into effect on 31 December
1989 and fills a regulatory void left after the 1984 expiry of the previous ordinance. The
islands expect to lose companies which fail to meet the stringent licensing
requirements, but the new law is intended to be flexible enough to attract legitimate
insurers while providing the means necessary to root out fraudulent companies.

279 **Turks and Caicos expects to pass new law.**
Deborah Shalowitz. *Business Insurance*, vol. 23 (April 10, 1989),
p. 73-74.
Shalowitz outlines the terms of a new law to regulate insurers and to provide for the
hiring of a permanent insurance supervisor. The new law was to be passed in late April
1989.

280 **Turks managers optimists despite setback.**
Robert A. Finlayson. *Business Insurance*, vol. 20 (April 14, 1986), p. 88.

Finlayson points out that regulations are needed to give the captive insurance industry legitimacy and to allow the Turks and Caicos Islands to compete with other countries. Although these controls, promised several years earlier, are not yet in place, managers are optimistic that the controls will be established since the British government agreed to provide funds to hire a commissioner of insurance to undertake this task.

281 **Drug arrest busts Turks and Caicos' plans.**
Robert A. Finlayson. *Business Insurance*, vol. 19 (April 15, 1985), p. 76-77.

Finlayson describes the problems faced by captive insurers following the indictment of the Turks and Caicos' Chief Minister, Norman Saunders, in Miami on drug trafficking charges in March 1985. He speculates that this incident could delay indefinitely efforts by the government to adopt a new ordinance that would place tighter controls on captive insurance companies.

282 **Turks and Caicos hope to tighten rules.**
Len Strazewski. *Business Insurance*, vol. 18 (April 2, 1984), p. 57.

Strazewski outlines a new ordinance which will tighten the rules governing insurance companies in the Turks and Caicos Islands, allow for tax-exempt insurance companies, and create a superintendent of insurance.

Salt

283 **The Turks Islands salt trade and industry: an historical economic geography.**
Anthony Gregory.   MA thesis, University of California, Berkeley, California, 1970.

Bermudians began taking salt from the uninhabited Turks Islands in 1678 and traded with the English northern colonies in America. The Turks Islands salt was an important element in Bermudian carrying trade until about 1750. By 1800, Turks Islands salt dominated the salt trade and the most prosperous years were from about 1805 to 1830. Emancipation, in the mid-1830s, was a serious blow to the salt industry. Gregory examines the physical environment of the Turks and Caicos Islands, the physical and cultural aspects of solar salt manufacturing, the beginnings of the Turks Islands salt industry, and the rise and decline of this industry in the islands. Gregory's use of the term Turks Islands refers to Grand Turk Island, Salt Cay and South Caicos Island. Although not available from University Microfilms, Ann Arbor, this thesis can be obtained from the University of Florida Libraries in Gainesville and the University of California, Berkeley.

284 **Salt industry in Turks and Caicos Islands.**
F.W. Fraser. *Commercial Intelligence Journal*, vol. 47, no. 1485 (July 16, 1932), p. 99.

Fraser gives an explanation of the salt collecting process and discusses the three types of salt produced in the 1920s and 1930s: coarse salt, fishery salt and three-quarter ground salt. He also provides production and export figures for 1930.

285 **Some salt islands of the West Indies.**
Chris H. Tice. *Chamber's Journal*, 7th series, vol. 6, no. 293 (July 8, 1916), p. 511-12.

Tice provides a poetic description of the Turks and Caicos Islands and a practical description of the process of salt production. At the time this article was written three settlements were engaged in salt production: Grand Turk Island, Cockburn Harbour, and Salt Cay. The United States and Canada were almost the exclusive consumers of the salt from the islands.

286 **Tùrks and Caicos Islands: report on the salt industry.**
Frederick H. Watkins. London: HMSO, 1908. 41p. (Great Britain. Colonial Office. Colonial Reports – Miscellaneous, no. 56).

Watkins was Commissioner of the Turks and Caicos Islands from 1906 to 1914. His report is divided into three parts. In Part I (p. 3-4), he outlines the chief facts and dates connected with the salt industry from 1678 to 1907. Part II (p. 4-28) is a short but excellent history of the salt industry and, of necessity, the islands themselves. Part III (p. 28-41) contains information on the process of salt raking, and provides a variety of statistics for the industry and some of the author's own general observations.

Sponging

287 **Report on sponges and the sponge industry in the Turks and Caicos Islands.**
Frederick H. Watkins. Kingston: Government Printing Office, 1913. 9p.

In this brief report, Watkins, Commissioner of the Turks and Caicos Islands from 1906 to 1914, provides a great deal of information about sponges and sponging. The report gives a physiological description of sponges and a description of how sponges are harvested. The document also includes a report by E.J.D. Astwood outlining the suitability of the creeks and inlets of Middle Caicos Island for the cultivation of sponges.

Philately and Numismatics

288 **Turks and Caicos currency.**
Mendel L. Peterson. *The Numismatist*, vol. 71 (March 1958), p. 268-74.

Peterson gives a history of the islands and the currency used since the time of the Bermudian salt rakers. The article includes photographs of Jamaican, British, American and Canadian coins, all of which have circulated in the islands at one time or another, as well as Turks and Caicos pound and five shilling notes.

289 **The postage stamps of the Turks Islands.**
Edward Denny Bacon. London: Stanley Gibbons, 1917. 32p.

Bacon outlines the history of the postal system in the Turks Islands and gives a great deal of information about the first eleven issues of postage stamps (1867-95). These first issues were all inscribed 'Turks Islands'. It was not until 1900 that this was replaced with the inscription 'Turks and Caicos Islands'. A twelve-page supplement was published in 1936 (London: Stanley Gibbons, 12p.).

Environment

290 **Take a coral island and crystal clear water – then dump on it.**
Robert Gordon. *New Statesman*, vol. 112, no. 2889 (Aug. 8, 1986),
p. 6.

Gordon describes a proposal by Applied Recovery Technology, Inc. of Philadelphia to
enter into an $18,000,000 per year contract with the British government to permit the
American company to dump sewage on uninhabited West Caicos Island. Gordon
sounds a strong ecological warning but admits the money would help to balance British
grants paid to the Turks and Caicos Islands on an annual basis.

291 **Parks and conservation in the Turks and Caicos Islands: a report on the
ecology of the Turks and Caicos with particular emphasis upon the
impact of development upon the natural environment.**
Carleton Ray, Alexander Sprunt. Grand Turk: [n.p.], 1971. 45p.
3 maps.

Ray and Sprunt have produced a summary of the ecology of the Turks and Caicos
Islands and their inshore waters with recommendations for the preservation of the
environment upon which the welfare of the islands depends. This work contains
sections on ecology, the results of aerial surveys and underwater investigations,
development principles, and parks and reserves. The authors make twelve recommendations including the establishment of parks and reserves and the need for integrated
land/sea conservation.

Statistics

292 **Statistical yearbook of the Turks and Caicos Islands.**
Turks and Caicos Islands. Government Statistical Unit.   Grand Turk:
Government Statistical Unit, 1989-. annual.
This annual provides a variety of statistics for population, education, health, employment, crime, fisheries, construction, transportation and communications, foreign trade, tourism, banking, public utilities, national income, land and property transfers, finances and prices. In many cases, statistics are given for a range of years, not just the current year under discussion.

Education

293　**Schools need major overhaul.**
Turks & Caicos Current, (Jan./Feb. 1984), p. 50, 52, 55.
This article outlines a number of activities being undertaken by the government to upgrade the educational system following the 1983 Collister Report, a British Development Division report on education in the Turks and Caicos Islands. The article also provides a number of statistics for student enrolment, examination passes and trained/untrained teachers.

Literature Set in the Turks and Caicos Islands

294 **The island.**
Peter Benchley. Garden City, New York: Doubleday, 1979. 302p.
A writer for an American news magazine investigates the disappearance of hundreds of boats carrying more than two thousand people. He and his son are kidnapped in the Caribbean and taken to a remote island in the Turks and Caicos where the bulk of this fairly implausible story unfolds.

295 **Dildo Cay.**
Nelson Taylor Hayes. Boston, Massachusetts: Houghton and Mifflin, 1940. 329p.
Hayes tells the story of Adrian Ainsworth who takes over the family's salt business on his father's death. Torn between his duty to maintain the business and his love of a beautiful woman, Ainsworth must come to a decision about his life and the future of his family's business.

Libraries

296 **Victoria Library is a public service now – but it wasn't always.**
Daphne James. *Turks & Caicos Current*, vol. 2, no. 6 (March/April 1985), p. 42-45.
James provides a fascinating but all too brief history of Grand Turks' Victoria Jubilee Library built in 1887.

Newspapers and Periodicals

Newspapers

297 Turks and Caicos News.
Grand Turk: Turks and Caicos News, 1982-. weekly.
This weekly reports local events with little or no international news.

298 Early printers of Grand Turk.
Roderick Cave. *Bibliographical Society of America. Papers*, vol. 70, no. 4 (Oct. 1976), p. 519-28.
In his article, Cave describes the history of the early newspapers, government printing practices, and rivalries between the newspapers and their publishers. These early newspaper publishers not only produced newspapers for the Turks and Caicos Islands, but also met the islands' printing needs. Prior to 1845 the printing needs had been met in the Bahamas and Bermuda. The first paper established was the *Turks Island Gazette and Commercial Reporter* which was published by Samuel Nelmes from 1845 to 1848. This first paper was followed by *The Royal Gazette and Turks Islands Commercial, Literary and Political Journal* (1849-57), the *Royal Standard and Gazette of the Turks and Caicos Islands* (1854-1907), and the *Weekly Record* (1892-94).

Periodicals

299 The Islands' Sun.
Providenciales, Turks and Caicos Islands: The Islands' Sun Times Ltd., 1989-. irregular.
This magazine, which appears to have had a tentative start, offers articles on the economy, business, lifestyle and history of the islands including memoirs and profiles

of Turks and Caicos Islanders. It is available from The Islands' Sun Times Ltd., 1859 N. Pine Road, #113, Plantation, Florida, 33322-9932, USA.

300 **Times of the Islands.**
Providenciales, Turks and Caicos Islands: Times Publications, 1988-. quarterly.

This glossy magazine, with its excellent photography, provides information on travel, business and finance, real estate, and the islands in general. It is primarily a magazine for people who do not live in the Turks and Caicos Islands, rather than an informative magazine for permanent residents. It is available from Times Publications, P.O. Box 234, Providenciales, Turks and Caicos Islands, British West Indies.

Directories

301 **Dictionary of Latin American and Caribbean biography.**
Ely, England: Melrose Press, 1970-. irregular.
This 'who's who' provides one alphabetic sequence of individuals by surname. There is no geographic access though the foreword indicates that individuals from the Turks and Caicos Islands are included.

302 **Personalities Caribbean: the international guide to who's who in the West Indies, Bahamas, Bermuda.**
Kingston: Personalities, 1965-. biennial.
This straightforward 'who's who' is revised every two years. There is no separate section for the Turks and Caicos Islands, but individuals from the island group are included under 'General Listing' with individuals from Belize, Cuba, the Dominican Republic and Haiti.

Bibliographies

303 **The Bahamas.**
Compiled by Paul G. Boultbee.   Oxford: Clio, 1989. 197p. map.
(World Bibliographical Series, vol. 108).
The 703 entries in this annotated bibliography have been grouped into thirty-five categories covering a wide range of subjects. Although the Turks and Caicos Islands are geographically a part of the Bahamas, there is no political connection and they have not been specifically considered. However, there are a number of entries which directly or indirectly refer to the Turks and Caicos Islands. Because of this and the islands' historical connections with the Bahamas, this bibliography does prove useful.

304 **Bibliography of the natural history of the Bahama Islands.**
William T. Gillis, Roger Byrne, Wyman Harrison.   Washington, DC: Smithsonian Institution, 1975. 123p. map. (Atoll Research Bulletin, 191.)
This bibliography lists, alphabetically by author, nearly 1,650 citations in twenty-two subject divisions, one of which is the Turks and Caicos Islands. Although the other subject divisions deal specifically with the Bahamas, many of the items listed will have some relation to the Turks and Caicos Islands. There are neither annotations nor indexes.

305 **Bahamas.**
Compiled by Norman William Posnett, Philip Miles Reilly.   Surbiton, England: Land Resources Division, 1971. 74p. (Land Resource Bibliography, no. 1.)
The 619 unannotated entries in this bibliography are almost exclusively journal articles and government documents from the 1960s. There are a number of references to government documents from Great Britain which refer to the Turks and Caicos Islands. Also, many of the Bahamian materials are related. There is a concentration on the environmental sciences, agriculture and forestry.

Index

The index is a single alphabetical sequence of authors (personal and corporate), titles of publications and subjects. Index entries refer both to the main items and to other works mentioned in the note to each item. Title entries are in italics. Numbers refer to bibliographic entries.

Map of Turks and Caicos Islands

This map shows the more important towns and other features.

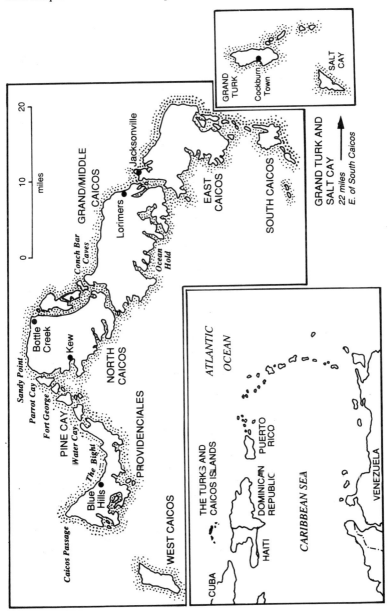